The Master's Plan for Making Disciples

Other Books by Win Arn and/or Charles Arn

Back to Basics in Church Growth
Catch the Age Wave
The Church Growth Ratio Book
Growth: A New Vision for the Sunday School
How to Grow a Church
How to Start a New Service
Live Long and Love It
The Pastor's Church Growth Handbook (v. 1)
The Pastor's Church Growth Handbook (v. 2)
Ten Steps to Church Growth
Who Cares about Love?

The Master's Plan for Making Disciples

Every Christian an Effective Witness through an Enabling Church

SECOND EDITION

Win Arn and Charles Arn

A Division of Baker Book House Co
Grand Rapids, Michigan 49516

Second edition published 1998

Published by Baker Books
a division of Baker Book House Company
P.O. Box 6287, Grand Rapids, MI 49516-6287
Sixth printing, August 2004

Printed in the United States of America

Library of Congress Cataloging-in-Publication Data

Arn, Win.
The master's plan for making disciples : every Christian an effective witness through an enabling church / Win Arn and Charles Arn. — 2nd ed.
p. cm.
Includes bibliographical references.
ISBN 0-8010-9051-2 (pbk.)
1. Evangelistic work. 2. Church growth. I. Arn, Charles. II. Title.
BV3790.A736 1998
269'.2—dc21 97-35109

For information about academic books, resources for Christian leaders, and all new releases available from Baker Book House, visit our web site:
http://www.bakerbooks.com

Contents

Introduction

In the beginning the early church grew—with megapower!

The events are recorded in the Book of Acts . . . from 12 . . . to 120 . . . to 3,000 . . . to 5,000 . . . from addition to multiplication . . . to entire communities turning to the Lord. Then the church was off on its globe-circling mission—a mission given by the head of the church, Jesus Christ, to disciple the many diverse peoples who make up the human family.

Through the centuries, the church has grown . . . grown among alien cultures . . . grown among hostile religions . . . grown among both primitive and sophisticated peoples. The church has triumphed over traitors, persecution, famine, and sword.

The Church's one foundation is Jesus Christ her Lord;
She is His new creation, by water and the Word:
From heaven He came and sought her, to be His holy
bride;
With His own blood He bought her, and for her life He
died.

Elect from every nation, yet one o'er all the earth,
Her charter of salvation, one Lord, one faith, one birth,

One holy name she blesses, partakes one holy food,
And to one hope she presses, with every grace endued.

'Mid toil and tribulation, and tumult of her war,
She waits the consummation of peace forevermore;
Till with the vision glorious her longing eyes are blest,
And the great Church victorious shall be the Church at
rest.

"The Church's One Foundation"
Samuel J. Stone

The church of Jesus Christ has grown, and continues to grow, to complete the task—a task yet unfinished.

As the church has grown in innumerable ways and places, there has always been one way it has grown better, faster, and stronger than any other. From its beginning, through the centuries until today, one unique way has been more responsible for the church's growth than any other. It is about this way—and the important implications it has for you and your church—that this book was written.

What about Today? The State of Evangelism

But while the church has grown—and there are more Christians today than ever before in the history of the world—there is still a vast unfinished task. Throughout the world three out of every four people have yet to believe. In the United States, out of a population of approximately 266 million, there are nearly 192 million pagans or marginal Christians (Christians in name only). Around every church in every community, there are winnable people waiting to be won. In fact, never in history has the worldwide potential for evangelism and church growth been greater. Yet that one way that God has used and blessed so greatly through the centuries seems to be strangely lacking in modern evangelistic endeavors.

Evangelism is not well. In fact, the lack of results through evangelism, compared with the task yet to be accomplished in America, should cause Christians both apprehension and concern. And it is as a direct result of the impotency in disciple making today that this book and supportive material have been researched and developed.

The Lord's words to his followers two thousand years ago remain unchanged for his followers today. His commands have not been updated, nor have they been revoked. "Go therefore and make disciples of all the nations, baptizing them in the name of the Father and the Son and the Holy Spirit, teaching them to observe all that I have commanded you; and lo, I am with you always, even to the end of the age" (Matt. 28:19–20).

But what about today? How do today's Christians view this biblical mandate? Is the goal of making disciples still at the center of the activities and prayers of Christ's church?

During the last twenty-five years, in traveling across America, ministering in churches, conducting seminars, holding consultations, conferring with church leaders, having discussions with laity, it has been our privilege to feel the pulse of modern evangelism. Based on our wide experience across the Protestant denominational spectrum, we have observed some important characteristics of evangelism in America.

1. Evangelism Is a Low Priority for Most Churches

What was once the heartbeat of the entire church, particularly the early church, has diminished enormously as a priority in the minds of its members. What was once an important criterion for success[1] has diminished to merely one item (and not a particularly important one) on the church's busy agenda. Church activities have become increasingly inward-focused. Events planned, money raised and spent, roles and jobs created are conducted primarily as a service to members and for maintenance of the organization. Leith Anderson observes, "It is not uncommon for churches more than twelve years old to not even want newcomers."[2]

Evangelistic activities, visitation programs, and witness training hold little enticement for the average congregation. Outreach functions are relegated to a small and usually impotent committee. Making disciples has become, in most congregations, a compartmentalized function, isolated from the mainstream of church thinking and life.

Contributing to this decline in priority is the fact that many laity and clergy no longer see the church as the instrument to reach the world. They mistakenly believe that the television and radio airwaves, the nationwide media blitzes, or the mass-evangelism rallies are the only effective way to respond to the Great Commission and reach the millions of unreached. Few perceive their own congregation as having the potential for being God's instrument to reach their community.

2. *Evangelism Is a Low Priority for Most Christians*

Very few laypeople feel able to effectively share their faith. When asked why they are a Christian and a church member, many can mumble little more than, "Well, it's a good thing to be." Not that they aren't enthusiastic about the reality of Christ in their life; they just have never been helped to communicate their faith. Most Christians today lack the training that would enable them to share with a non-Christian, in a natural, effective way, what Christ means to them.

While many laity feel inadequate in expressing their Christian beliefs, some are even unsure of what they believe. "Christian in name only" typifies nearly one-half of all the people today who call themselves Christians.

3. The Biblical Concept of "Lostness" Has Disappeared

In our modern culture the understanding that people outside Christ are eternally lost—once a theological imperative—has changed in the minds of many believers. The reasons behind this are varied and complex. They may range from a world influenced primarily by situation ethics to a general erosion of confidence in the Scripture. However, many believers tend to perceive lostness only in a sociological dimension, neglecting the spiritual dimension. For many, lostness has little to do with the biblical concept of eternal separation from God.

Little remains of the first-century Christian's burning conviction that without Christ every person is forever lost. Nor is there that fervent zeal for non-Christian friends and relatives that swept across America as great evangelists graphically portrayed the terrifying damnation of a godless eternity. Today's Christians are not convinced of the reality of this foundational concept of Christianity.

4. Few Evangelism Methods Make Disciples

The bottom line following evangelism efforts is, Does the church grow? In many churches there are more people leaving through the "back door" of attrition (transfer, death, reversion) than there are new Christians coming in the "front door" as a result of evangelism programs. That is not to say that churches aren't growing—some are. They just aren't growing as a result of evangelism programs.

Local congregations, sincere in their efforts to reach out with the gospel, often import a program or formula that has seemingly been successful in other churches. The methods widely used often attempt to compact a life-transforming gospel presentation into a fifteen-minute or less visitation call. In the process little consideration is given to the unique needs of the individual. The non-Christian has a very limited opportunity to discuss the consequences of this major step of faith. No significant relationships are established. Non-Christians seldom if ever have a chance to observe the realities of Christ in the lives of Christians. And often there is no effective plan to incorporate the new convert into the life of the local congregation. Indeed, some evangelism methods even encourage callers not to mention the church in their conversation.

5. Evangelism Focuses on Decision Making, Not Disciple Making

Most approaches to mass and local church evangelism today have a significant common shortcoming. Attention is centered around, and success judged according to, the goal of "getting a decision." That brief verbal commitment is seen as the ultimate response to the Great Commission. Unfortunately, there is often a great gap between getting a decision and making a disciple. The latter suggests a commitment, incorporation into the body, then an ongoing, reproductive lifestyle as a follower of Christ. An analysis of many church training programs and parachurch crusades in America today indicates that the bottom line for evangelism is the number of decisions recorded. This decision-making mentality may be one of the reasons national church membership continues to decline, in relation to population growth, in spite of so much being said and done in mass evangelism, media evangelism, evangelism training, and evangelism conferences.

6. Making Disciples Is Interpreted to Mean Only Spiritual Growth

In the Great Commission, Jesus makes clear that the command to "go and make disciples" includes the concept of "winning." Today "discipling" has evolved to mean the process of spiritual perfecting—tutoring, learning, growing, maturing. Few discipling programs in churches today accurately reflect Christ's vision to make disciples or are measured for success on the basis of new disciples produced.

While the concept of spiritual maturation is unquestionably important, an exclusive emphasis on spiritual growth often serves as an undesirable magnet pulling a Christian's focus increasingly inward as concern for those outside the body of Christ progressively decreases. In such a self-centered environment, the goal of fulfilling the Lord's Great Commission moves lower and lower as a priority.

7. Evangelism Methods Have Become Simplistic

There is strong evidence to indicate that people who accept Christ and continue as responsible church members first perceive the gospel message in terms of its relevance to their lives. Evangelism training that relies on canned presentations, memorized testimonies, and spiritual dictums does not prepare the believer to respond to the unique needs of the non-Christian in terms of his or her day-to-day experience and the resources available in Christ. Dr. Arthur Glasser, noted theologian in the field of church growth, observes, "People today must see Jesus Christ as the liberator from injustice, transformer of human culture, as well as personal Savior of the human heart."[3]

8. Evangelism Is Much Discussed but Little Practiced

The following parable speaks insightfully of the problem of much talk but little effective action.

> Now it came to pass that a group existed who called themselves fishermen. And lo, there were many fish in the waters all around. In fact, the whole area was surrounded by streams and lakes filled with fish. And the fish were hungry.
>
> Week after week, month after month, and year after year these, who called themselves fishermen, met in meetings and talked about their call to go about fishing.
>
> Continually they searched for new and better methods of fishing and for new and better definitions of fishing. They sponsored costly nationwide and worldwide congresses to discuss fishing and to promote fishing and hear about all the ways of fishing, such as the new fishing equipment, fish calls, and whether any new bait was discovered.
>
> These fishermen built large, beautiful buildings called "Fishing Headquarters." The plea was that everyone should be a fisherman and every fisherman should fish. One thing they didn't do, however; they didn't fish.
>
> All the fishermen seemed to agree that what is needed is a board which could challenge fishermen to be faithful in fishing. The board was formed by those who had the great vision and courage to speak about fishing, to define fishing, and to promote the idea of fishing in far-away streams and lakes where many other fish of different colors lived.
>
> Large, elaborate, and expensive training centers were built whose purpose was to teach fishermen how to fish. Those who taught had doctorates in fishology. But the teachers did not fish. They only taught fishing.

Some spent much study and travel to learn the history of fishing and to see far-away places where the founding fathers did great fishing in the centuries past. They lauded the faithful fishermen of years before who handed down the idea of fishing.

Many who felt the call to be fishermen responded. They were commissioned and sent to fish. And they went off to foreign lands . . . to teach fishing.

Now it's true that many of the fishermen sacrificed and put up with all kinds of difficulties. Some lived near the water and bore the smell of dead fish every day. They received the ridicule of some who made fun of their fishermen's clubs. They anguished over those who were not committed enough to attend the weekly meetings to talk about fishing. After all, were they not following the Master who said, "Follow me, and I will make you fishers of men"?

Imagine how hurt some were when one day a person suggested that those who don't catch fish were really not fishermen, no matter how much they claimed to be. Yet it did sound correct. Is a person a fisherman if year after year he/she never catches a fish? Is one following if he/she isn't fishing?[4]

So What about Today?

How does this present state of evangelism compare with the New Testament state of evangelism? Interestingly, there were significant differences in the early church:

1. Reaching non-Christians was a high priority for the church. Indeed, the very "call to arms" of Christ for his church was to reach out and make disciples.
2. Reaching non-Christians was a high priority for individual Christians. It was an assumption that every Christian was to be a committed witness to Christ's love.

3. The concept of lostness was foremost in the minds of Christians and churches. Christians believed wholeheartedly that Jesus Christ was the way, the truth, and the life.
4. Evangelism methods were designed to make disciples. Peter, Paul, Philip, Barnabas, Mark—the success of their endeavors was measured by the growth of the church and by the number of new disciples. Throughout the Book of Acts we see the growth of the church and the multiplication of disciples.
5. Evangelism focused on disciple making, not decision making. Nowhere in Scripture will you find the concept of getting a decision. The bottom line was a transformed life and an active Christian—a disciple.
6. Making disciples meant reaching non-Christians and then teaching them how to grow spiritually and how in turn to make more new disciples. Christ said it best when he said to go and baptize new disciples and then teach them all he had taught. First reaching, then teaching—the two went hand in hand.
7. Evangelism methods presented the whole gospel and its implications. When people made a Christian commitment, they knew the price they might have to pay.
8. Evangelism was the priority of the church. And Christians were Christ's witnesses in Jerusalem, Judea, Samaria, and to the uttermost parts of the world.

Are we, as Christians, simply to wait for our Lord's return, with no concern for those people still outside God's family? Of course not! Disciples are commissioned—as much today as they were by Christ himself. What is more, the harvest fields are ripe across North America and throughout the world. Awareness and receptivity are increasing. Old frustrations resulting from years of failure are bringing a new and desperate plea: "Show us a better way!"

Are churches catching the vision and seizing the opportunities for making disciples? Growth is indeed occurring in some congregations, where members are actively involved in sharing God's love and building his body. Excitement and enthusiasm are permeating churches where the fellowship of believers lovingly incorporate new Christians.

God is not going to be defeated! Jesus Christ is not powerless! God is the Father Almighty. The church has abundant resources and excellencies, and evidences a strength and goodness no other organization dares to dream of. The facts indicate that the church is expanding and will continue to do so.

But how can more Christians and more churches respond to this opportunity for making disciples? The future is bright for any church dedicated to fulfilling the Great Commission. *But there must be a fresh beginning!* Old methods have not brought, and will not bring, in the catch waiting just outside the boat. There is a better way, a creative and enjoyable and effective way for you and your church to bring in a net that will be full beyond your most fervent prayers and greatest expectations.

We believe that the strategy reviewed in this book uses the powerful principles of disciple making exemplified and called for by our Master. *The Master's Plan for Making Disciples* seeks to identify, illustrate, explain, and apply for you and your church both principles and practices that have produced and will continue to produce abundant results in the lives of individuals and churches—for the glory of God and the growth of his church!

1 The Master's Plan: Making Disciples

Wearily Chuck Bradley turned to his wife. "Diane, I'm not going . . . and that's final!"

"But I promised you'd go with me," replied Diane.

"Don't I have the right to make up my own mind?"

"Well, sure you do, sweetheart, but I just assumed you'd be interested in learning more about evangelism."

"Please, Diane, don't try to make me feel guilty!"

"But just think how it will look if I go alone. People will say, 'Chuck Bradley doesn't care about sharing his faith.'"

Chuck did not like the direction this conversation was taking. "You know that's not true. I do care about evangelism, as much as anybody. I just don't care about another 'witnessing seminar.'"

"But Pastor Austin said this would be different."

"Well, of course he'd say that. I'm just tired of trying to learn one new method after another for witnessing. You'd think we were some kind of door-to-door salespeople."

"But you do believe that Christians ought to share their faith?"

"You know I do . . . but I'm just not sure Jesus should be marketed by people acting like used-car dealers. Besides, I haven't had much success with those kinds of methods, anyway. Remember the summer we went camping and I tried out my new witnessing training? Why, a couple of people even agreed to make a decision. And then—"

Diane interrupted. "Yes, I know. You overheard one of them saying later that the way to get rid of those missionary types is to say yes so they'll go away and leave you alone."

"I really heard that, Diane."

"A few bad experiences shouldn't give you the right to stop witnessing."

"You're absolutely right. But at this moment I have a very hard time believing that anything I say as a witness will really make a difference in another person's life."

"But if you go with me tonight, maybe you'll learn something that will help," pleaded Diane.

"No. When it comes to witnessing, I feel just like those disciples who fished all night and caught absolutely nothing!"

How do you feel about witnessing? Or sharing your faith? There are a lot of Christians who feel like Chuck. Although they believe in evangelism, what personal efforts they have made produced little or no results. Like the disciples, many Christians feel they have "fished all night and caught nothing."

But remember, that's not the end of the story. Let's refresh our memories.

The first rays of the morning sun peek over the sunburned eastern hills. Stretching out for miles below lies a quiet, mirrorlike blue lake. A few hundred yards offshore, a solitary boat seems fastened to the still surface. Occasionally one of the two figures in the twenty-foot wooden boat stands and stretches. The motionless air carries a rooster's wake-up call across the water.

Finally the men begin to pull in their nets, causing ripples of water to make their way toward shore. The sound of water dripping from nets being pulled to the surface breaks the morning silence as the fishermen eagerly search their nets for the product of the long night's labor. But as the last of the empty nets pile onto the boat bottom, the men dejectedly reach for the oars. Another wasted night.

"How's the fishing?" a man calls from shore.

After a pause a frustrated voice replies, "Nothing. Absolutely nothing!"

"Throw your nets on the other side of the boat," orders the man on shore.

"But we've fished all night." Then, after a long pause and sensing an authority in the man's voice, the fisherman responds, "All right, but only once more."

A short time later, after the fishermen have again let out their nets into the same water, shouts of excitement ring out. From the boat sound calls for help—help to pull in nets so full they are beginning to break!

What a moment that must have been! Peter and Andrew trying desperately to bring in the catch, excitedly shouting to their fellow fishermen. Yet what mind-stretching questions must have been racing through their heads! How had Jesus, from the shore, known where the fish were? Was it a miracle? It must have been! But how? Why?

As they pull the wiggly, flopping fish into the boat, the words Jesus had spoken to Peter long ago suddenly echo in his mind: "Follow Me, and I will make you fishers of men" (Matt. 4:19).

During his life on earth our Master gave us a plan for successful fishing, a model for making disciples. There is a vast potential catch available on "the other side of the boat" if we follow his plan. It is a plan that can result in many new people coming into a life-changing relationship with Christ and his church, a plan that results in a new spiritual dimension in our own lives . . . new effectiveness in making disciples . . . new ministry and growth for our churches in fulfilling his command to "go and make disciples."

The Master's Plan: God's Purpose

"For God so loved the world, that He gave His only begotten Son, that whoever believes in Him should not perish, but have eternal life. For God did not send the Son into the world to judge the world, but that the world should be saved through Him" (John 3:16–17).

But how could the world that God so loved ever hear and believe such an awesome act of love? Jesus, in a conversation with his Father, supplies the answer: "As you have sent me into the world, so I have sent them into the world . . . that the world may believe that you have sent me" (John 17:18, 21 NRSV). The Lord made his disciples' task crystal clear: "You shall be My witnesses both in Jerusalem, and in all Judea and Samaria, and even to the remotest part of the earth" (Acts 1:8).

What were they to witness about? Again Christ was specific and direct: "Thus it is written, that the Christ should suffer and rise again from the dead the third day; and that repentance for forgiveness of sins should be proclaimed in His name to all the nations, beginning from Jerusalem. You are witnesses of these things" (Luke 24:46–48).

God, speaking to us through Scripture, presents a startlingly clear statement of his desire and unswerving purpose that lost humanity be reached and brought into his fellowship. Christ's birth, crucifixion, and resurrection were for the purpose of reconciling men and women with their Creator. Passage after passage in the Bible clearly underscores God's will that "all men . . . be saved and . . . come to the knowledge of the truth" (1 Tim. 2:4).

The Master's Plan: The Commission

In a final summary of his earthly life and purpose, Christ turned over his commission from God to his followers. As his Father had sent him, so he was sending them (John 20:21). It was a life-encompassing challenge that could not be misinterpreted: "Go therefore and make disciples of all the nations, baptizing them in the name of the Father and the Son and the Holy Spirit, teaching them to observe all that I commanded you" (Matt. 28:19–20).

This commission to his followers, repeated on several occasions, reflects God's eternal purpose that all people everywhere have the opportunity to become disciples of Jesus Christ. It was this command of God through Jesus Christ that exerted singular direction on the early church. When Christ gave the church this final directive, there was no question but that this command was to be given top priority.

Central in all Christ's teaching was the assumption that to follow him meant to become participants in his mission. Christ did not accept the idea of a sideline disciple.

The expectation that all who received Jesus Christ as Lord and Savior would become his faithful and active disciples appears to have been widely held by first-century Christians. What the apostle Paul affirmed they assumed was true of themselves: "We are ambassadors for Christ, as though God were entreating through us; we beg you on behalf of Christ, be reconciled to God" (2 Cor. 5:20).

Being Christ's follower assumed not only a commitment to his lordship but also an involvement in the propagation of his gospel. By definition disciples became "fishers of men." Christ's central desire for his disciples was that when he was gone, they would have ingrained in their hearts and minds the conviction that the Son of Man had come to seek and to save those who were lost. His words, now called the Great Commission, were simply a restatement of his entire life and teaching, as he endeavored to make the matter as simple and easy to understand as possible: "Go and make disciples."

The Master's Plan: Make Disciples

The words of Christ in Matthew 28:19–20 communicate vividly Christ's understanding of a disciple. He saw a disciple as one who becomes a follower, who is taught, who is nurtured in the faith, who in turn goes out to make disciples, who are then taught and nurtured in the faith, who then in turn go out.

The perpetual multiplying of disciples reflects Christ's strategy for reaching "the remotest part of the earth" (Acts 1:8). This strategy, as Luke records, became the basis of the explosive growth of the early church: "The number of disciples was multiplying" (Acts 6:1 NKJV); "And the number of disciples multiplied greatly in Jerusalem" (Acts 6:7 NKJV); "The churches . . . were multiplied" (Acts 9:31 NKJV).

Christ expects every disciple to be a witness. Witnessing to the Good News is simply the expression of Christian discipleship. Acts 1:8 provides an important key to Christ's expectations of his disciples. He said, "You shall be My witnesses." The Greek verb in this command is actually in the declarative form. Had Christ used the imperative verb *to be,* it would have implied a conscious activity or planned action. Rather, Christ meant that *being* his witness was to be a natural, assumed part of the disciple's lifestyle. This normal dimension of the disciple's life is God's secret to fulfilling the Great Commission!

The Master's Plan and the Early Church

The early church shared the gospel so people all around the world would have faith in Christ and obey him (Rom. 16:26). And Luke records that people did respond in faith and obedience: "The word of God kept on spreading; and the number of the disciples continued to increase greatly in Jerusalem, and a great many of the priests were becoming obedient to the faith" (Acts 6:7).

What principles caused those first-century Christians to achieve such remarkable success in making disciples? Why were the early Christians described as "people who have been turning the world upside down"? (Acts 17:6 NRSV).

1. The Goal Was Clear: Make Disciples

Being a disciple in the early church meant a firsthand involvement in the mission of Christ—making disciples. The goal was clear and all-encompassing.

An important facet of the early church's disciple-making goal was to continually expand this base of new disciples. In the book *Back to Basics* the authors note that "inherent in being saved was that the redeemed share the Good News. Being a Christian meant worshipping God; it meant doing good to all people, especially those of the household of faith. It meant expecting the Lord to return. It meant sins forgiven. *But above and beyond these, it meant telling people that the Savior had come*—that eternal life was theirs by believing in Him—that believing gave them the right to become children of God."

A new convert's commitment to Christ included the assumption that disciples reproduce themselves and continue the disciple-making chain. New disciples were instruments used by the Holy Spirit in making disciples. Noted mission strategist George Peters observes that "the total program of indoctrination was designed to *make disciples* as [the apostles] had been instructed by their Master to do. For the apostles, this meant to equip the believer for the ministry of their calling (Ephesians 4:11–16), and to qualify them to give intelligent and reasonable answers for the hope that was in them (I Peter 3:15)."[1]

2. Every Christian: A Witness

Inherent in the definition of a disciple was the idea that one shared the Good News with others. For the early Christians, making disciples was not seen as a compartmentalized activity or the responsibility assigned to a designated few. Rather, by its very nature it was an integral part of the lifestyle of every believer. In observing the characteristics of the New Testament church, a noted church historian has observed that "every member was mobilized and actively involved . . . all functioned as responsible members in the body life of the church."

First-century Christians told the story of Christ simply and graciously. Each believer's actions and attitudes confirmed the centrality of Christ in life. Christians vouched for the way the Lord had met all their needs. As Christians enthusiastically exemplified how the realities of Christ were a consistent part of everyday experiences, they presented a convincing witness. Naturally and winsomely, these Christians told of "the hope that was within them."

In the video *The Great Commission Sunday School* Donald McGavran provides an insight into this contagious spread of the gospel: "Some of the greatest growth of the church took place when refugee Christians spread out across Judea. The Bible says, 'They preached the Word.' Well, they didn't stand up in pulpits and preach. They met people as they fled from Jerusalem and told them about Jesus."[2]

A Disciple Is . . .

The Lord's mandate to his church rings loud and clear: "Make disciples." What is a disciple? What is the process by which one becomes a disciple? What are the characteristics of a disciple? Read the following verses, then briefly answer the related question.

1. What Is a Disciple?

- *A disciple is a believer.* How does one become a believer? (John 11:25–26; Acts 16:30–31)
- *A disciple is a follower.* How does one become a follower? (Matt. 16:24; John 13:15)
- *A disciple is a learner.* What are the marks of a learner? (John 8:31–32; 2 Tim. 2:15)
- *A disciple is a witness.* To what does he or she witness? (Mark 5:18–19; 1 Peter 3:15)
- *A disciple is baptized.* How does baptism express a disciple's commitment? (Acts 2:38, 41–42; Acts 22:16)
- *A disciple is a reproducer.* What is a disciple to reproduce? (Matt. 28:19; John 15:8)

2. List Two Characteristics of a Disciple, Given in John 8:12 and 13:35

3. Write a Definition of a Present-Day Disciple

Although fellowship with members of the body was a vital part of the believer's life, they did not remain in the "holy huddle." Scripture records that everywhere they journeyed, early Christians witnessed to the claims of Christ. While there are only three references in the New Testament to those who are "evangelists" (with the special gift of evangelism), Scripture contains over 120 references to the broader commission to all members of the church to preach the gospel and make disciples. The early Christians did not discount the command of making disciples simply because they lacked the gift of evangelism. Witnessing to their new faith was a lifestyle of every Christian and every church. By naturally communicating their faith, they became God's instruments for bringing many people into his kingdom.

3. Compassion: Permeating the Mission

The early Christians knew the deep concern their Lord had for "lost sheep." Jesus expressed his divine love even toward the unloved. He loved Matthew and Zacchaeus, the despised tax collectors; he loved Roman centurions, the hated overlords of Judea; he loved lepers; he loved the blind, the lame. Christ's love for the multitudes, the children, the outcasts of society, must have been told and retold by the first believers.

The early church mirrored its Master's compassion. Koinonia was one of the church's hallmarks: Its members jointly participated in the life of Christ in their midst. The church was a loving, caring community. These first-century Christians expressed compassion in the daily routines of everyday living: the many garments Dorcas made and gave to the poor (Acts 9:39); the sharing of property and possessions as anyone had need (Acts 2:45).

In writing to the Corinthians, Paul warned with those often repeated and sometimes uncomprehended verses, "If I speak with the tongues of men and of angels, but do not have love, I have become a noisy gong or a clanging cymbal" (1 Cor. 13:1). Compassion was a fruit of the Spirit. Compassion was one of the seeds of New Testament church growth.

4. Relationships: The Means for Sharing the Master's Love

While the goal of the early Christian was, as Christ had commanded, to make disciples, there was a process by which the early church grew so explosively. The means of church growth was through the individual Christian's interlocking social system—his or her family, friends, and associates. Christ often commanded new believers to return to their "households" (friends and family) and tell them the Good News. Noted scholar Michael Green, in *Evangelism in the Early Church,* observes that the New Testament church religiously adhered to the strategy of using households in the Christian advance.[3] Luke records how those in the homes of Christians responded to the gospel, with the result that "the Lord was adding to their number day by day those who were being saved" (Acts 2:47).

Why were these households of friends and family so receptive to the gospel? Two reasons: First, the caring and love that characterized the household relationships implied a level of trust, friendship, and common concern. In the household a person's concerns and convictions were respected and heard. Second, those intimate with the new believer could witness the reality of a life changed by the power of the Master's love. Such a change in a person's lifestyle naturally had a significant impact on one's friends and family.

The early Christians knew that when the message of God's love was heard and demonstrated by those who were known and trusted, the barriers of distrust and suspicion lowered and receptivity to the Good News increased tremendously. Thus the members of the early church continued Christ's example of making new disciples, as the Good News of God's love moved quickly and naturally along the lines of relationships.

5. Receptive People: The Point of Concentration

Christ left no doubt concerning the importance of concentrating on receptive people. In the parable of the sower, Jesus illustrated the concept of receptivity as he explained that the seed sown on good soil is the person who both hears and understands the message. Such a person's life shows a good crop of thirty times, sixty times, or a hundred times what was sown (Matt. 13:23). There seemed no doubt in Christ's mind that the "seeds" should be planted in "fertile soil."

The apostle Paul utilized the pattern of focusing his evangelistic activity on responsive people. He was so convinced of the importance of preaching Christ to people who were receptive that he asked the Colossians to pray "that God may open up to us a door for the word, so that we may speak forth the mystery of Christ" (Col. 4:3). In Corinth God told Paul, "I have many people in this city." God wanted him to concentrate on the city of Corinth because there were many responsive people there (Acts 18:8–11). In Ephesus Paul writes, "But I will tarry in Ephesus until Pentecost. For a great and effective door has opened to me" (1 Cor. 16:8–9 NKJV).

Scripture also records the results of preaching to receptive people. "And when [Paul and Barnabus] had arrived and gathered the church together, they began to report all things that God had done with them and how He had opened a door of faith to the Gentiles" (Acts 14:27).

The disciple-making efforts of the early church were fruitful, and the church grew, as a result of its members communicating the gospel to clearly receptive segments of the population—whom God had prepared!

6. *The Master's Plan: Directed and Empowered by the Spirit*

The early Christians knew their source of strength—the Holy Spirit, who empowered them to live up to the high calling left by Christ Jesus. The Holy Spirit is revealed as the great strategist throughout the Book of Acts. He is indisputably the Superintendent of the great missionary endeavor. He empowers and initiates, guides and directs. George Peters observes that "as the goal of the church seen in Acts 1:8 gradually unfolded, the Holy Spirit surely motivated the church in its onward movement. On the day of Pentecost believers received the baptism of the Holy Spirit."[4]

Evidence of this direct effusion and guidance of the Spirit abounds in the Book of Acts. One recalls how Philip, after having been significantly used by the Spirit to bring many Samaritans to Christ, was guided to reach an Ethiopian eunuch with the gospel (Acts 8:29).

And the beginnings of the evangelization of the Gentiles was likewise under the Spirit's direction: "While Peter was reflecting on the vision, the Spirit said to him, 'Behold, three men are looking for you. But arise, go downstairs, and accompany them without misgivings; for I have sent them Myself'" (Acts 10:19–20).

The Holy Spirit continued as an active part of the spread of the gospel: "And while they were ministering to the Lord and fasting, the Holy Spirit said, 'Set apart for Me Barnabas and Saul for the work to which I have called them'" (Acts 13:2).

The pages of the New Testament tell again and again of men and women who by faith in Jesus Christ were given access through the Spirit to the Father. Filled with unshakable certainty that God had, through Christ, opened the way of salvation, they multiplied churches throughout the land.

The Holy Spirit not only directed the mission of the early church, he also empowered believers to accomplish their Christ-ordained mission. The Lord Jesus told them to wait for the Holy Spirit because he would give them power to be witnesses in Jerusalem, Judea, Samaria, and the uttermost parts of the world. The Holy Spirit provided the power to fulfill the mandate Christ had given them: "And with great power the apostles were giving witness to the resurrection of the Lord Jesus, and abundant grace was upon them all" (Acts 4:33).

7. Boldness: In the Extension of the Faith

In the forum in Rome, in Ephesus, in Lystra, the Scriptures do not portray Paul possessed with the spirit of compromise or timidity (Eph. 6:19). Instead, we read of the courageous yet loving proclamations made here and there by an ambassador of the one true God. Paul preached his message fearlessly, even though he was frequently mobbed, beaten, and ridiculed.

Boldness was no more a natural or inherent trait of the early Christians than it is today. The apostles needed to pray often to God, asking for boldness in preaching (see Acts 4:29).

"And when they had prayed, the place where they had gathered together was shaken, and they were all filled with the Holy Spirit, and began to speak the word of God with boldness" (Acts 4:31). The early believers did not shrink from trial or hardship. In its face they prayed for boldness. And Scripture testifies to the fruits of this intense desire to communicate the Good News no matter what the cost. "Now when they saw the boldness of Peter and John, and perceived that they were uneducated and untrained men, they marveled" (Acts 4:13 NKJV).

8. The Scriptures: A Reference Point

Concerning the New Testament church's use of the Scriptures, Michael Green observes, "As these first-century Christians preached the Good News, one phrase 'the Word' seems to be the heart of what they communicated. Wherever they went these early believers spread the Word. So much so that when Luke means us to understand that the church expands, he tells us that the Word grew. The Word means, of course, their proclamation of Jesus on the basis of the Old Testament."[5]

The apostles, grounded in the Old Testament Scriptures, knew that their Jewish audience regarded the Scriptures as absolute truth. The phrase "for it is written" held the potential for convincing even the Jewish skeptics. Again and again these disciple makers pointed to Christ's birth, life, death, resurrection, and ascension as the fulfillment of the Old Testament prophecy, proclaiming that God's eternal promise to reconcile humanity to himself had at last been fulfilled (Acts 13:32–35).

In dealing with those of Jewish background, early Christians made frequent use of verses or passages from Scripture. It is clear, from their quotation of the Old Testament, that they had a strong preference for particular passages—Psalm 110 was the most favored of all. They immersed themselves in the Word they proclaimed. They gave themselves to studying and thinking out how they would proclaim this Word.

The early Christians knew that God, who had spoken partially through the Old Testament Scriptures, had now spoken fully and completely through Jesus Christ. So the believers searched the Old Testament Scriptures for insights concerning the Messiah.

9. The Church: A Body of Believers

The New Testament frequently pictures the disciple of Christ in a group setting: a sheep in a flock, a soldier in an army, a limb in a body, a stone in a building. Being a member of the early church was a corporate experience. "They worshiped together regularly at the Temple each day, met in small groups in homes for Communion, and shared their meals with great joy and thankfulness, praising God" (Acts 2:46 TLB).

The early church recognized that by meeting together, the body derived strength, encouragement, stimulation, and knowledge. "Let us hold fast the confession of our hope without wavering, for He who promised is faithful . . . not forsaking our own assembling together, as is the habit of some, but encouraging one another; and all the more, as you see the day drawing near" (Heb. 10:23, 25).

For those first-century believers, there were no "see you next week" farewells or the expectation for any member to "go it alone." The growing number of disciples gave personal attention to each other's needs in the context of everyday living. No one was forgotten. Their faith had given them a mandate to love one another. Now they were putting it into action!

The television was blaring as Diane opened the front door. In front of the set Chuck was sleeping soundly. Diane turned off the television, bringing Chuck out of his sleep.

"Diane, you just got home?"

"Just walked in the door," answered Diane. "Sweetheart, you really missed a good meeting."

Chuck sat up, took off his glasses, and tried rubbing the sleep out of his eyes.

"And what new evangelism techniques did you learn?"

"It wasn't like that."

"Oh, come on, admit it. You learned three new methods for buttonholing people for Jesus. In fact, your purse is probably packed with new 'miracle tracts' guaranteed to make people instant Christians."

Diane was exasperated. "Believe me, we didn't even talk about methods of witnessing. What we studied was the early church and their strategy for disciple making."

Chuck stood up. "Can't you see what Pastor Austin's doing? He's setting you up. And next week you will learn what evangelism methods were used by the early church—and how we can use them today. Right?"

"You're probably right. But maybe we should learn to use their methods. After all, didn't they turn their world upside down?" Diane gave Chuck a parting smile and headed for the bedroom.

"But Diane . . ."

It was too late. She was gone and the discussion was over.

2

How New Disciples Are Made: The *Oikos* Factor

"Joshua, a Jewish merchant from Rome, walked briskly along the cobblestone road. He knew, as he passed more and more people, that he was getting closer. He had heard much and thought often about the City of David—as had every Jew throughout the Roman world. Forty years earlier Herod the Great had begun a major restoring project in Jerusalem to return it to its former grandeur. Not since the time of King Solomon had such palaces, citadels, amphitheaters, viaducts, and public monuments been built. So magnificent were these buildings Herod had begun that some were still being completed. Joshua had heard that visitors were overwhelmed by the city's splendor."

Chuck restlessly changed his position. Pastor Austin was reciting another one of his fictional, quasi-biblical narratives, and Chuck wasn't interested.

"The winding road made its way over a hill of gnarled olive trees. Joshua's pulse quickened. His pace increased. As a Jewish merchant, he had officially made this trip for business reasons. But secretly Joshua had always longed for a reason to take the several-week journey from Rome to Jerusalem and see the city of his dreams. Nearing the top of the last hill, he no longer noticed or nodded to travelers passing on the road. He was sure that on the other side of the hill . . . He broke into a run, sandals clapping against the cobblestones.

"Then he saw it. He gazed, transfixed. Joshua could not believe he was actually there. Across the valley, set among the surrounding hills, was Jerusalem—'the perfection of beauty,' in the words of Lamentations, 'the joy of all the world.'"

Why, Chuck wondered, had he let Diane talk him into coming to session 2 of Pastor Austin's seminar "Disciple Making: The Master's Plan"? Was it because Diane had been so insistent? Or was it because as a committed Christian, he carried guilt feelings about his lack of fruitfulness as a witness for his Lord?

"As Joshua approached the city, he could see how the massive stone wall that surrounded it had been damaged, repaired, and enlarged over the centuries. At intervals along the wall were located massive gateways through which people streamed in and out of the city. Just inside each gate was a customs station, where publicans collected taxes on all goods entering and leaving the city. Joshua explained his mission to the gatekeeper and was told to report to the customs center near the temple, where an officer would explain the regulations.

"Once inside the city, Joshua faced a bewildering maze of dusty, winding streets and alleyways. As he pushed through the crowds, slowly making his way toward the temple, his senses were assaulted by the odor of bread baking and the sounds of voices raised in bartering or in song, the braying of donkeys, the bleating of sheep soon to be sacrificed. In the excitement Joshua nearly forgot to ask directions to his brother-in-law Benjamin's house, where he would be staying while in Jerusalem."

Chuck glanced at Diane. She was far away . . . with Pastor Austin in first-century Jerusalem. Chuck discreetly checked his watch. When would the pastor get to his point? Who cares about some imaginary Jewish merchant from two thousand years ago?

"The next day Joshua spent as a tourist walking through the city. Since it was the holiday feast of Pentecost, most merchants were not doing business. As Joshua entered the marketplace, he noticed a gathering on the far side of the court. It seemed to be a political meeting or a public debate.

"Walking closer, Joshua saw a large, bearded man standing above the others, speaking to the crowd. Suddenly Joshua's heart jumped. He couldn't believe what he was hearing. The Jewish man was speaking in fluent Latin, a language Joshua had not heard since he left the Roman ship on the coast of Israel. He listened.

"The man speaking called himself Peter and spoke of strange but fascinating things. Peter spoke of the Messiah foretold by the prophets and said that this Messiah had already come. In fact, Peter claimed that he had been with the Messiah only days before! Peter's message filled Joshua with a strange sense of intrigue. It was unthinkable that the Messiah had come. Everyone would know! Yet the story this man told sounded reasonable and compelling. Could the long-awaited Messiah actually have come?

"Later that day Joshua responded to Peter's message about the risen Christ and his love. Joshua and three thousand others were baptized. He hurried home to tell Benjamin and his family of this exciting new dimension to the Jewish faith. That night as Joshua, overflowing with joy, shared the events of the day, Benjamin, Benjamin's wife, Miriam, and their whole family made the decision to follow Jesus, the Messiah.

"To learn more about his new faith, Joshua stayed in Jerusalem longer than he had planned. He, Benjamin, and Miriam joined the other believers as they devoted themselves 'to the apostles' teaching and to fellowship, to the breaking of bread and to prayer' (Acts 2:42).

"Joshua wrote home to his wife, Ruth, and their children to explain his delay. He told them of his new faith and sent the letter by Ananiah, a friend in Rome, who was visiting Jerusalem and who also became a disciple at Pentecost.

"By the time Joshua returned to Rome, his family had already become disciples of Jesus the Messiah. Between Joshua's letter and Ananiah's personal testimony, they couldn't resist this faith that fulfilled and completed their Jewish beliefs. Joshua began sharing the apostles' teaching with his family and with Ananiah. Soon Ananiah's family and servants also came to the Lord.

"Meanwhile Joshua returned to his import-export business. He gathered his employees to tell them of this new faith. Many of them believed and asked Joshua to help them share the Good News with their families.

"Whether he knew it or not, Joshua was part of a process of making disciples that would be the way the Christian movement would eventually become the most widespread faith and force on earth. And a key element in that process was the communication of God's love through an established network of social relationships that the Greek New Testament calls 'oikos.'"[1]

Almost imperceptibly Chuck shook his head. Doesn't Pastor Austin realize that we don't live in the first century? What may have worked then doesn't necessarily work today!

Chuck's question about the applicability of two thousand-year-old principles deserves an answer. But first let's examine the meaning of the new word *oikos* introduced by Pastor Austin.

Oikos is the Greek word for "household." In the Greco-Roman culture, oikos not only described the immediate family in the house but included servants, servants' families, friends, and even business associates. An oikos was one's sphere of influence, his or her social system composed of those related to each other through ties of kinship, tasks, and territory.

The Household and the Old Testament

The Old Testament pictures the household (*bayit* in Hebrew) as including several generations in a family. In the book *Anthology of the Old Testament* Hans Walter Wolff observes that "a household usually contained four generations, including men, married women, unmarried daughters, slaves of both sexes, persons without citizenship, and 'sojourners,' or resident foreign workers."[2] Old Testament Scripture confirms again and again the significance and uniqueness of the household and the family. God's original promise to Abraham included the provision that through him "all the families of the earth shall be blessed" (Gen. 12:3). The word *families,* according to noted biblical historian Cornell Goerner, "does not refer to the simple family unit composed of a man, his wife, and their children, but rather describes the extended families, or the oikos."[3]

Later God directed his people, "In the presence of the LORD your God, you and your families [bayit] shall eat and shall rejoice in everything you have put your hand to, because the LORD your God has blessed you" (Deut. 12:7 NIV).

There are many other references to the centrality of the family and household in the lives of God's people: "And there rejoice before the LORD your God, you, your sons and daughters, your menservants and maidservants, and the Levites from your towns" (Deut. 12:12 NIV).

"Then you and your household shall eat there in the presence of the LORD your God and rejoice" (Deut. 14:26 NIV). "And the family which the LORD takes shall come near by households" (Josh. 7:14).

Oikos and the New Testament

God continues to focus on the household (friends, extended family, associates) in the New Testament in his plans for communicating to humankind. The Gospels, Acts, and the Epistles show that the bridges of oikos were used regularly as a means to spread the Good News. After healing a demon-possessed man, Jesus told him, "Go home to your friends [oikos] . . . and tell them what wonderful things God has done for you; and how merciful he has been" (Mark 5:19 TLB).

After Zacchaeus was converted, Jesus said to him, "Today salvation has come to this house [oikos]" (Luke 19:9).

When Jesus healed the son of a royal official, "he and all his household [oikos] believed" (John 4:53 NIV).

Levi followed Jesus and invited his fellow tax collectors—his oikos—to come to dinner, and as a result many followed Christ (Mark 2:14–15).

The apostle Peter came to Christ as a result of someone in his oikos: "The first thing [Andrew] did was to find his brother Simon. He said to him, 'We have found the Messiah'" (John 1:41 NEB). And another disciple, Nathaniel, came to Christ as a result of his friend Philip, who "went to find Nathaniel, and told him, 'We have met the man spoken of by Moses in the Law'" (John 1:45 NEB).

Following Christ's resurrection and ascension, it was this same pattern of the gospel moving through the oikos that caused the early church to explode. Noted church historian Kenneth Scott Latourette has observed that "the primary change agents in the spread of faith were the men and women who earned their livelihood in some purely secular manner, and spoke of their faith to those whom they met in this natural fashion."[4]

In the Book of Acts, chapter 10, the story is recorded of the first non-Jewish household to respond to the message of the apostles. It took a special vision from God to convince Peter that it was all right to tell Gentiles about Christ. But when the invitation came from the centurion Cornelius, Peter was ready. When he and several other believers arrived, they found Cornelius "had called together his relatives and close friends [his oikos]" (Acts 10:24). Scripture records that when Peter finished sharing the gospel, the entire household responded (Acts 10:44). Later, as Peter tried to convince the Jewish Christians in Jerusalem that the gospel could also be for the Gentiles, he told of the vision from God and the call from Caesarea, where he went and spoke and an entire household was saved (Acts 10–11).

In another example, Paul and his companions shared Christ with a businesswoman named Lydia, outside the city of Philippi. The Bible records that she responded to their message and that she and the members of her household were baptized (Acts 16:15).

Shortly thereafter Paul and Silas were thrown into jail. As they were praying and singing hymns, an earthquake freed all the prisoners from their chains. Rather than face death because of the escaped prisoners, the jailer prepared to kill himself. But Paul assured him they were still there, and the jailer asked, "Sirs, what must I do to be saved?" They replied, "Believe in the Lord Jesus, and you shall be saved, you and your household. And they spoke the word of the Lord to him together with all who were in his house [oikos]. . . . And immediately he was baptized, he and all his household. . . . and [he] rejoiced greatly, having believed in God with his whole household" (Acts 16:31–34).

Donald McGavran, founder of the modern church growth movement, observed that believers in the early church had relatives and friends scattered across the Roman Empire. "According to the record, some of the Christians who had first spoken of the faith to Greeks in Antioch came from Cyprus. They probably belonged to families who had connections on both the island and the mainland. Having converted their relatives in Antioch, it was natural for them to think of reaching their unconverted relatives, Jews and Greeks, in Cyprus."[5] Even as the new Christians were thinking of their relatives, the Holy Spirit was preparing Barnabus and Saul for a missionary trip that would begin in Cyprus. As the Antioch congregation discussed the Lord's leading and made arrangements for the trip, people with relatives along the proposed route would surely have made suggestions. In the book *Bridges of God* McGavran recreates the scene.

> Some Jewish woman in Antioch may have said to Paul: "I have a brother in Iconium. He has, for many years, longed for the coming of the Messiah. How I wish it were possible for him to hear you! He has a large house and has prospered in business. He would give you a genuine welcome. Do let me send him word."
>
> Wherever he went, Paul must have had someone's brother-in-law or second cousin or aunt or uncle to look up. He could approach such a person with a message: "Simon sends his greetings, and says to tell you the family is well. He hopes you and your household are well, and he said that you might like to hear the message we bear, that the Messiah has come and brought a new way of life."

> Think of the great receptivity such contacts would have produced! It is, to us, an inescapable inference that Paul at Antioch must have known of many such relatives and must have realized their enormous importance in the extension of the faith.[6]

Paul was not the only one spreading the gospel. Thousands of Christians were telling friends and relatives in their oikos about Jesus. In the video *But . . . I'm Just a Layman* the observation is made, "You probably think the phenomenal growth of the early church took place because of a few dedicated apostles. Absolutely not! It grew explosively because of the laity—ordinary men and women telling their friends and family about Jesus Christ and the Good News of salvation."[7]

Michael Green observes, "The early Christians knew that when the message of faith was heard and demonstrated by friends and family who were known and trusted . . . receptivity to the Gospel increased tremendously."[8]

Chuck could wait no longer. He raised his hand. "But Pastor, what basis do we have for assuming that this oikos concept works today?"

Diane was a little embarrassed by Chuck's bluntness, but Pastor Austin didn't seem to mind the question. "Good question. I think the best way to answer that would be to take a few minutes and share some of the various ways some of us have come to Christ and to this church. Who will be first?"

An older woman in the front row raised her hand. Standing, she told the group how she was now in the church because of a friend from church who lived in her mobile home park. This friend invited her to attend some meetings in the women's circle. She came to the meetings and in time made a Christian commitment. She continued as an active Christian and member of the church even after her friend passed away.

A younger woman, about twenty-five, told how she came to Christ through her Christian parents. When she moved to this community to take a job, she began looking for a church. A friend of hers at work was attending this church, so it was a natural step into the church after she visited a few times.

A middle-aged man then told how one of his cousins, who lived in town, introduced him and the family to Christ and this church.

"Chuck, does that answer your question?"

"Yeah, I'd say that answers it." Chuck turned to Diane, who gave him an "I told you so" smile.

The Importance of Oikos Today

Webs of *common kinship* (the larger family), *common friendship* (friends and neighbors), and *common associates* (work associates and people with common interests or recreational pursuits) are still the paths most people follow in becoming Christians today.

Research conducted by Church Growth, Inc. of Monrovia, California, supports the notion that the oikos process is at work today. Over forty-two thousand laypeople were asked the question, What or who was responsible for your coming to Christ and your church? One of the following eight responses was given:

1. Some said a "special need" brought them to Christ and the church.
2. Some responded they just "walked in."
3. Some listed the "pastor."
4. Some indicated "visitation."
5. Some mentioned the "Sunday school."

6. Some listed "evangelistic crusade or television show."
7. Some recalled that the church "program" attracted them.
8. Some responded that a "friend/relative" was the reason they are now in Christ and the church.

What percentage of people gave each response as to how they came to their new relationship with Christ and their church? Here are the results.

Response	Percentage
Special need	1–2%
Walk-in	2–3%
Pastor	5–6%
Visitation	1–2%
Sunday school	4–5%
Evangelistic crusade or TV show	½%
Church program	2–3%
Friend or relative	75–90%

The conclusion is clear: The majority of people today can trace their "spiritual roots" directly to a friend or relative. (Do some research in your church to see if this holds true.)

Here are some examples of how people come to Christ and the church today.

The Prince of Peace Lutheran Church in Carrollton, Texas, where Dr. Steve Wagner is pastor, is typical. Two members of the church, husband and wife, invited a non-Christian neighbor couple to their church's family enrichment program. The couple enjoyed a pleasurable and positive experience. Later the husband and wife invited these non-Christian friends to a Sunday morning worship service, and the couple continued to attend together. Soon the wife made a commitment to Christ. She enrolled their four-year-old boy in the church's preschool program. A few months later her husband came to Christ, and they joined the church. Following their commitment, the new Christian mother encouraged a friend of hers to enroll her four-year-old in the church's preschool program. And at the next family enrichment program, the new Christian couple brought a non-Christian friend and the wife's brother. The brother began attending a Sunday morning worship service, enrolled in a church membership class, and has since become a Christian. He in turn is sharing his faith with his parents.

This natural web of relationships has quickly resulted in eight people making professions of faith and becoming responsible church members. And the web of growth is just beginning.

Another example: A sales manager and member of Ness Avenue Baptist Church in Winnipeg reached two members of his oikos (two work associates) for Christ and the church. The pastor of the church has since identified thirty-four people that have come to Christ from this web of oikos members.

In the Grove City, Ohio, Church of the Nazarene there is a program, built around oikos, called "The Family Tree." It began as a result of a young couple coming to Christ and the church and afterward being responsible (either directly or indirectly) for bringing thirty-five other adults (plus thirty-two children) to Christ and the church.

Figure 1 illustrates the oikos phenomenon as traced in a Free Methodist church in Bellingham, Washington. It started with a young man named Ron Johnson. Look at the relationships over which the gospel traveled. (Names and ages when they became a Christian are given.)

The centuries-old concept of oikos, or webs, continues to be the bridge over which the Good News of God's love naturally travels.

Figure 1

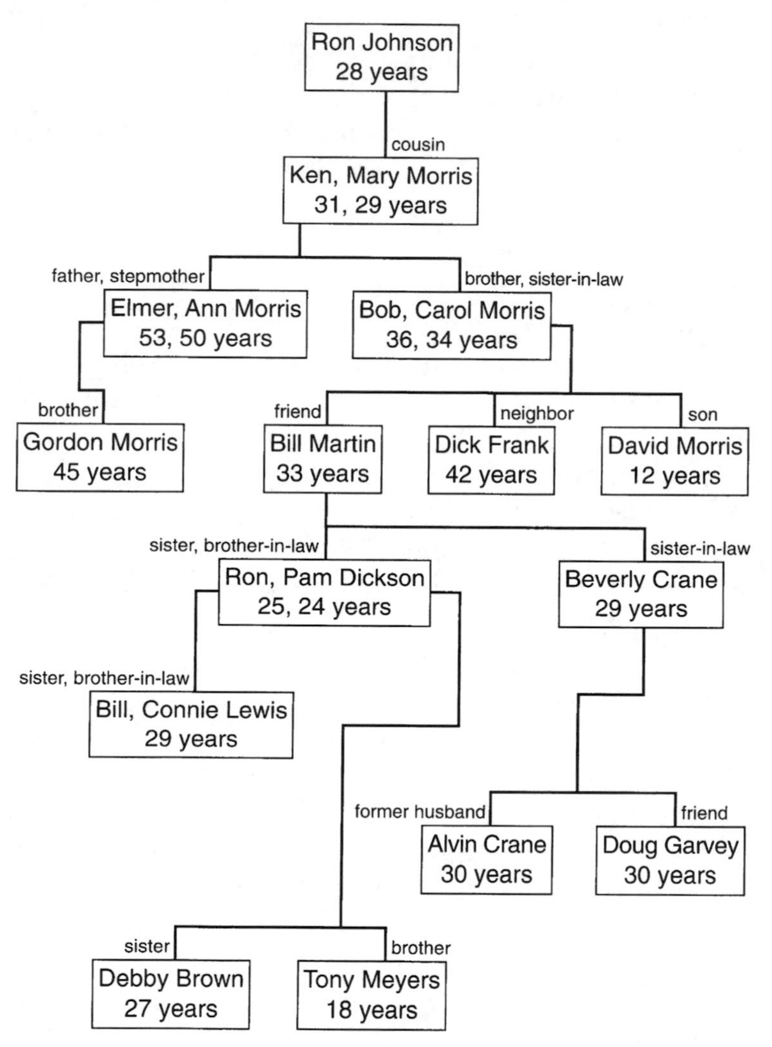

Ron Johnson
28 years
cousin
Ken, Mary Morris
31, 29 years
father, stepmother
Elmer, Ann Morris
53, 50 years
brother, sister-in-law
Bob, Carol Morris
36, 34 years
brother
Gordon Morris
45 years
friend
Bill Martin
33 years
neighbor
Dick Frank
42 years
son
David Morris
12 years
sister, brother-in-law
Ron, Pam Dickson
25, 24 years
sister-in-law
Beverly Crane
29 years
sister, brother-in-law
Bill, Connie Lewis
29 years
former husband
Alvin Crane
30 years
friend
Doug Garvey
30 years
sister
Debby Brown
27 years
brother
Tony Meyers
18 years

Why Oikos Is Effective

Why do people respond so positively to the gospel as it travels over webs of relationships?

1. Oikos Relationships Are a Natural Network

The new Christian, who has discovered the joy of experiencing God's grace, is naturally eager to tell others. He or she wants close friends and relatives to share in this new freedom and joy. The oikos of friends, relatives, and associates is the most natural place for new Christians to share their newfound joy with others—those people who mean the most to them.

"I believe Nancy and Susan are good examples of how the oikos principle has worked in our church," Pastor Austin said, smiling at two young women in the second row. "Susan, would you mind sharing with the group how you and Nancy became disciples?"

"Sure," said Susan. "Nancy and I had been roommates for a little over a year. We got along well together and enjoyed each other's company. Neither of us were Christians, so it came as quite a shock to me one day when she came home and started talking about having committed her life to Jesus Christ."

2. Oikos Members Are Receptive

There is quite a difference between hearing the witness of a trusted friend and hearing a "religious presentation" from a stranger. When God's love is discussed with an oikos member, that person is usually open and receptive, since he or she is listening to the experience of someone they know and trust.

"I remember," continued Susan, "that when Nancy began explaining her new attitudes and belief, I was really interested. She still seemed to be normal—I mean, she hadn't suddenly freaked out or anything." Susan laughed and looked at Nancy. "And talking with her in our apartment, I felt comfortable asking questions and discussing her new ideas and faith."

3. Oikos Relationships Allow for Natural Sharing

Relationships with oikos members are by their very nature regular and natural. Whether members are on a social outing or in the comfort of a living room, the relationships are usually easy and relaxed. And the Christian lifestyle demonstrates Christ's love in a variety of places, times, and situations. Communicating the gospel is not squeezed into one short visit or presentation. Being a witness to the life-changing effects of God's love over a period of weeks, months, and even years allows the oikos member time for thoughtful consideration about becoming a disciple.

"Although I was interested, I needed time to think about what it all meant," said Susan. "I had a lot of preconceived notions about what a Christian was and did, and I needed some time to see what Nancy's new commitment really meant to her. As days and months went by, I saw some significant changes in Nancy, and being around her and seeing what her faith meant to her had an important effect on my own thinking."

4. Oikos Relationships Support the New Christian

When a friend or relative comes to faith, there is a natural source for nurture and encouragement. Since at least one Christian—the original web member—is close to the new convert and eager to see growth in his or her life in Christ, new Christians are not left alone. There is someone to love, care for, and nurture them.

"After three months I began attending some church events with Nancy," Susan recalled. "Six months later I decided to commit my life to Christ. As a young Christian, it has meant a great deal to have Nancy's loving support as we grow together in our faith."

5. Oikos Relationships Effectively Assimilate Converts

It is natural for the new Christian to begin attending the church to which his or her friend or family member belongs. Because of this "bridge," the new Christian can easily become associated with other Christians in a Sunday school class or fellowship group and begin to build relationships within the body.

"I really feel at home in this church, although at first it was 'Nancy's church.' But soon it became my church, too. I joined the Sunday school class of which Nancy was a member, and met many new friends. The social activities sponsored by the church also helped me feel part of the group."

6. Oikos Relationships Tend to Win Entire Families

When one or two people in a family come to Christ and the church, it is often the beginning of a process that results in the entire family becoming new disciples. As the entire family grows together in Christ, the family unit is strengthened. On the other hand, if the entire family is not reached, conflict and fragmentation often result. Christians and non-Christians have different goals and priorities. Due to a lack of family support spiritual growth is more difficult, and the new Christian may drop out of an active Christian life. Once one family member has made a Christian commitment, an effort should immediately be made to identify and reach others in the family.

"After I made a commitment to Christ and joined this church," Susan concluded, "I immediately told my mother, brother, and sister-in-law of the exciting new discovery I had made. I'm hoping they too will soon discover the joy of being a Christian. Anyway, I'm praying for them."

7. Oikos Relationships Provide New Contacts

Each new person reached for Christ and the church has his or her own group of relatives, friends, and associates who are candidates for the Good News. Research shows that on the average each new Christian has twelve people in his or her oikos who are non-Christians. (Long-term Christians often have fewer; the average for most is about four.) In most cases everyone in a new Christian's web is outside Christ and a local church. The process of identifying receptive people and reaching out to them is never completed, because with each new Christian there are new contacts and opportunities.

Throughout the two thousand-year history of the church, God has richly blessed the church's growth through webs of oikos relationships. The oikos concept is timely yet timeless. It is planned yet not contrived. It is founded on solid research, experience, and principles found throughout Scripture. It is the way churches have grown and continue to grow, as each new oikos member who comes to Christ and the church has his or her own web of friends and relatives. And the pattern continues.

After the session Chuck cornered Pastor Austin with another question. "Wouldn't the gospel have spread faster," Chuck asked, "if the early church had been able to use modern media—like radio and television?"

Pastor Austin smiled and shook his head. "No, I don't think so. The first-century church had a better medium for communicating God's love."

"And what was that?"

"Well, it was what we talked about tonight—the oikos network. And Chuck, it's still the best medium."

3 Key Principles of Disciple Making

The bright morning sun had little effect on Chuck as he sat sipping his breakfast coffee. He had slept badly, tossing and turning most of the night.

"What's wrong, sweetheart?" asked Diane.

"I just can't do it."

"Can't do what?"

"I just don't think I can share my faith. And I know that I should! I lay awake most of the night thinking about it."

"But why do you feel that way?"

"Well, that's what I've been wrestling with. I think it's because I feel inadequate. I mean, who am I to explain the gospel to people? I've never even been to seminary!"

"But none of the apostles ever went to seminary. And they did pretty well at sharing their faith!"

"Yeah, but they were apostles. Besides, I'm not good enough. You know I'm not, Diane."

"Stop putting yourself down. Did you ever think what would have happened if the first Christians had waited until they were perfect before sharing their faith? The church would have died right in the first century."

Chuck nodded. "I never thought of that. But who would be interested in my witness?"

"What do you mean?"

"Well, you know how people are today. They're only interested in money . . . and things . . . and having a good time. No one's interested in the church . . . or my faith."

Diane placed her hand over his. "Chuck, you believe that your relationship to Jesus Christ makes a difference in your life."

"Well, sure. I wouldn't be a Christian if I didn't. That's what bothers me most. I would like to share my faith . . . if I could."

"God So Loved the World"

God's unswerving purpose is to reach out in love to humankind. He calls his church and each of his disciples to commit to see this happen. As we saw in the first chapter, this is the priority of Christ and the command to his church.

Most Christians and churches believe this. The problem comes when church leaders and laity try to translate this general call to arms into specific marching orders. "What can we, as a church or as individuals, do that is significant? And how do we do it?" Indeed, this shortage of practical guidelines for effective evangelism is one of the greatest frustrations in the church today. "'Go and make disciples'—fine, but how?"

It is for this reason that we are suggesting an important new approach to disciple making in and through the local church. It is an approach that builds on new church growth research previously unavailable to designers of evangelism programs. The new approach is not a program but a process—a process that builds on the natural webs of relationships that exist in every church. It is a process that can be a rewarding, fruitful experience for each participating church member. We call it The Master's Plan!

The Master's Plan is a unique merging of New Testament principles and modern church growth insights, designed to help you and your church effectively respond to Christ's Great Commission where he has placed you.

The Master's Plan is a strategy of disciple making to help lay church members identify and reach the people in their web, or oikos, for Christ and the church. It is a process that works within natural characteristics of human behavior and relationships and relates the unique needs of friends and relatives to Christ's work in their lives. The Master's Plan is a fulfilling, satisfying lifestyle for all church members. It is not an exercise in sweaty palms, stomach butterflies, or high degrees of anxiety but is one of the most enjoyable experiences a Christian will have in his or her lifetime—guaranteed!

In studying the example of Christ and the early church and in analyzing the church throughout history, we are convinced that when God has blessed the church with dramatic growth, it has occurred through the households and relationships and webs of people. The Master's Plan builds on the scriptural insight that the Christian message travels best over natural bridges of friendships and relationships—oikos. It is a disciple-making strategy that seeks to identify receptive people whom God has prepared and reach them while they are reachable.

The Master's Plan is based on the conviction that God wants his lost children found. The bottom line in effective evangelism is whether people are reached for Christ and the church grows. The motivation behind a concern for successful disciple making is the conviction that God desires his church to be effective in proclaiming the gospel and making disciples. The Master's Plan, when incorporated and practiced in the local church, is an intentional and powerful way to see this happen.

Principles of The Master's Plan

What is the foundation supporting this major new approach to disciple making in the local church? There are nine key principles in The Master's Plan disciple-making strategy. Here is a brief statement of each. (These principles are elaborated throughout the book.) As you consider this church growth model for disciple making, examine these principles closely. Study them. Test them with your experiences in evangelism and disciple making. Question them. Use them.

Principle 1

Disciple making is most effective when it is an intentional response by the local church to the Great Commission.

In many churches today the number of people, dollars, and time used for outreach forces one to conclude that in the natural course of church life there is little effort made to reach people.

Intentionality in evangelism is the church's response to Christ's command to make disciples. It is an act of obedience, an acknowledgment of his lordship. It means that disciple making becomes part of the priorities and goals of the church—part of its very reason for being. It means that the church regularly measures itself against the yardstick of the number of new disciples it produces. It means that the church makes a commitment to disciple making and sticks with it. It means that the purpose and activities of groups within the church include specific steps to bring new disciples into the local body of believers.

Such intentional evangelism does not automatically happen. In fact, churches often grow inward-focused over time, becoming more concerned with their own survival and less concerned with their call to reach out.

But is intentional evangelism merely a weekly calling program or a series of witness training meetings or the employment of a minister of visitation? Certainly some effort is better than none, yet research indicates that in a typical church only one to two out of every one hundred people came to the church as a result of a formal visitation program.[1] Intentionality in outreach means doing something, but it doesn't mean doing just anything. More than just good intentions are required. Effective evangelism requires insight and study as to what are the best and most productive intentional efforts that can be made. Some intentional efforts will be more effective in making disciples than others.

Effective disciple making combines intentional growth principles with an "evangelistic mix" that fits the local church and its unique situation. Tremendous power results in a local church that focuses on specific growth goals. When staff, lay leaders, groups, officers, and members determine to reach new people and grow, with God's help nothing will stand in their way.

Principle 2

Disciple making is most effective when focused on the oikos (natural networks) of existing Christians.

In church after church, denomination after denomination, across America and around the world, God uses friends, relatives, and associates as the primary means of reaching people. This has been the process, as we have seen, since the earliest days of the Christian church.

As we discussed in chapter 2, webs of common kinship (the larger family), common friendship (friends and neighbors), and common associates (work associates and people with common interests or recreational pursuits) are the means by which most people become Christians.

The fact that most people come to Christ and the local church through webs of relationships has important implications for your church. An effective disciple-making plan is one that builds on this solid foundation and allows God's love and salvation to flow over these bridges.

Here are eight important reasons why identifying and using natural networks of relationships should be the foundation for the outreach strategy of every church.

1. It is the natural way churches grow.
2. It is the most cost-effective way to reach people.
3. It is the most fruitful way to reach people.
4. It provides a constantly enlarging source of new contacts.
5. It brings the greatest satisfaction to participating members.
6. It results in the most effective assimilation of new members.
7. It tends to reach entire families.
8. It uses existing relationships.

Principle 3

Disciple making is most effective when based on and permeated with love and caring.

"This is My commandment, that you love one another, just as I have loved you. Greater love has no one than this, that one lay down his life for his friends" (John 15:12–13).

I remember being part of a ten-month consultation project in the Middle East. I lived alone on the bottom floor of a five-story apartment building. It was a cold and wet January. After having dinner at a corner restaurant, I walked home through a light snowfall and retired for the night.

About 3:00 A.M. I woke to a slight twinge in my stomach—it was trying to tell me something. Lying on that small, hard bed, I had an uneasy feeling that it concerned the potato salad I had eaten for dinner. By 4:00 A.M. my stomach was no longer hinting at a potential crisis. It was coming right out and announcing, "Friend, we have a problem!" By 5:00 A.M. there was no doubt that I was the recipient of a genuine case of food poisoning. I kept telling myself, "It's okay. Think about something else. It will go away," all the while secretly hoping against hope. But as seasoned foreign travelers know, food poisoning has a habit of not going away without a fight. I spent the remainder of the early morning plodding a path between the bed and the bathroom. By daybreak I could barely move. Sometime after noon, with much effort, I dressed and walked down the snow-covered street to a public telephone, called the office, and told them my situation. I said I would not be in—in fact, the way I felt, I was lucky to be alive!

The acute sense of isolation I felt as I stumbled back to my apartment is still vivid in my mind. There I was, half a world away from my home and family, in a strange city where I could not even speak the language. I was cold, wet, miserable, and felt that if I died, no one would ever know or care. I trudged slowly back to the apartment, stumbled through the entryway outside my room, and collapsed back in bed.

Some hours later I was awakened by the loud electric doorbell. Bzzzzz . . . bzzzzz. I walked slowly to the door. On the other side of the twenty-foot entryway that led outside the building, I saw two of the American team members with whom I worked, standing in the snow and waving to me. They had come in response to my earlier call. In my bathrobe I walked over and opened the door to a blast of cold air and snow. My friends had walked the two miles from their apartment to mine on that cold, snowy night to deliver their spirit of concern and a thermos of hot vegetable soup. It was one of the most touching moments of my life. Their caring and concern for me seemed unrepayable. I couldn't express what it meant. I wasn't alone. Someone cared. I was loved. What a world of difference it made!

Caring for people is a key distinction and quality of effective disciple making—a genuine expression of God's unconditional love. "For God so loved the world, that He gave His only begotten Son, that whoever believes in Him should not perish, but have eternal life" (John 3:16). God's love for his children is beyond question: "You must let little children come to me, and you must never stop them. The kingdom of Heaven belongs to little children like these!" (Matt. 19:14 PHILLIPS). Effective disciple making calls for each Christian who is a recipient of Christ's great love to become a channel through which that love can flow to those to whom Christ wants to give life eternal.

Caring: Allowing God's love to flow through you to people, especially those in your network of relationships.

God has seen fit to communicate his love to non-Christians through his representatives. "The one who loves God should love his brother also" (1 John 4:21). Christians are commissioned to represent Christ, and Christ's greatest quality is that of love (1 John 4:16).

The translation of Christ's love into tangible, specific action is the process of caring. Caring is spending time with a person. It is building a stronger and closer relationship. It is helping in a time of need, doing things for someone else that you would do for yourself. "We know that we have crossed the frontier from death to life because we do love our brothers. . . . My children, let us love not merely in theory or in words—let us love in sincerity and in practice!" (1 John 3:14, 18 PHILLIPS). Caring is loving. And we are called to love and care for one another.

"But I have called you friends, for all things that I have heard from My Father I have made known to you. You did not choose Me, but I chose you . . . that you should go and bear fruit, and that your fruit should remain. . . . This I command you, that you love one another" (John 15:15–17).

Principle 4

Disciple making is most effective when each Christian has a part in responding to the Great Commission.

Anyone can do it! Any church member who can identify an unchurched friend, relative, neighbor, or associate can be a disciple maker. As we have seen, the average church member has between seven and nine friends and relatives outside Christ and the church. Newer Christians and members of newer churches average twelve; older Christians and members of older churches average four. If a church of two hundred members had an average of six unchurched friends or relatives per member, the number of potential disciples would be one thousand two hundred! Even if there were an overlap of two hundred people, the church would still have identified one thousand who would be some of the most receptive people anywhere in that community. Since each church member is usually the best bridge into his or her web of relationships, making disciples becomes the concern of every member as they communicate God's love to these people.

This widespread lay participation in disciple making not only contributes to enlarged church outreach but also results in considerable side benefits. One such benefit is Christian maturity among participating church members and throughout the spiritual life of the body. Individual Christians actively involved in the Great Commission discover a sense of purpose and meaning in their Christian life. Perhaps for the first time they feel they are making a significant contribution to the cause of Christ. Being part of such a cause improves the self-image of a person and gives an important sense of spiritual self-worth. Participating in making disciples responds to that spiritual need.

How does spiritual maturity and growth occur in a Christian's life? What contributes to a growing, developing, maturing Christian? Is it daily prayer, regular Bible study, frequent participation in Sunday school and worship? Certainly, these are all important. Yet often we assume that spiritual growth occurs only in the context of such activities. Actually, it doesn't. In fact, when personal-growth-oriented concerns make up the entire experience of the Christian life and the church's programming, the result is to stunt the individual's spiritual growth and development. Why? Because participation in the very thing Christ desired most of his disciples—to make the Good News known—is ignored. Christlikeness can hardly be an achievable goal if there is no participation in the reason for Christ's mission.

It may be something like searching for happiness. People seldom find it by looking for it. They find happiness as a result of involving themselves in a task that is fulfilling and satisfying. Happiness is the result! The secret of spiritual growth may be not in the search but in the result, the result of commitment to a greater task of "bringing forth much fruit"—of making disciples.

Christ said it best: "Unless a grain of wheat falls into the earth and dies, it remains by itself alone; but if it dies, it bears much fruit. He who loves his life loses it; and he who hates his life in this world shall keep it to life eternal" (John 12:24–25). Participating in the process of disciple making may be as worthy for its role in the maturity of the Christian as it is in reaching the non-Christian. A Christian remains spiritually immature if he or she is not involved in the greatest task the Master called us to do.

Being part of productive disciple making is great spiritual therapy! It can spark the weariest Christians with a new flame of enthusiasm and excitement as they see new people—their friends and relatives—come into the joyful experience of the Christian life. Effective disciple making is a stimulus for renewal in personal growth and corporate morale.

Principle 5

Disciple making is most effective when it is a team effort.

I remember, as a boy, venturing down a narrow, four-foot-wide dirt tunnel that gradually descended deeper and deeper into the ground. A friend and I thought it would be an exciting adventure to find out where it went. I led the way. On hands and knees we made our way down the incline. About ten feet from the tunnel entrance we began a slight turn to the left, and soon the comforting light of day was lost. We groped farther and farther down along the darkened walls. I felt more and more isolated and alone. What if the tunnel collapsed? We would be stranded. No one knew where we were—they would never find us. I can vividly remember the hollow, empty sense of being alone. We both decided the adventure was not worth the anxiety or potential consequences, and we backed out!

I remember a similar feeling of isolation, apprehension, and separation when I was part of a witnessing program. A friend and I were given a list of names and addresses and sent out to call. I led the way. But as we left the security of the church and other members, I felt as if I were crawling down a deep, dark hole. We were removed from the comfortable security of the body and its members and sent to call on people we had never seen, people we didn't know, people who might be very hostile. If things went according to plan, we would give each person our memorized presentation and ask for a decision. If the person was not receptive, it was probably the last time he or she would hear from us. And if the person was not home, we would leave a door-hanger and depart.

Regardless of the outcome, the responsibility resting on our shoulders weighed heavily. I wondered, How can I, in a ten-minute call, represent all that Christ and my church mean to me? All the needs Christ can meet in a person's life? The joy of communion, fellowship, and growth with God's people? How can we communicate such things to strangers—strangers who may not be asking the questions we are going to answer? I felt as if my tunnel were about to collapse. I was isolated, even from my own church. I wanted to back out! There must be a better way!

God hasn't planned for us to be isolated. He has given us a community of brothers and sisters, a community whose whole is greater than the sum of its parts.

Why is a team effort more productive for disciple making than any one individual effort?

One reason is because each member has been given different gifts to build up the body (see Eph. 4:16). The concept of spiritual gifts is as old as the New Testament. Peter notes that each Christian has been given a gift (1 Peter 4:10). Paul says, "Now concerning spiritual gifts, brethren, I do not want you to be unaware" (1 Cor. 12:1). Numerous other passages throughout the Bible directly or indirectly refer to the fact that Christians are given gifts to use in the service of Christ's body.

While a detailed study of spiritual gifts will bring many new insights into the Christian life, the important insight for disciple making is that the variety of gifts God has given his church should play a central part in communicating the gospel. While no one person has all gifts, each Christian has at least one gift to be used in the body. Effective disciple making therefore means using your gift and then supplementing it with others' gifts in a team effort to build the body. All gifts can and should be used to help the church grow. Consider how the gifts of others in your church can be used to complement your own.

A second reason why a team effort will be more effective in disciple making is that the more and varied the contacts a non-Christian has with the body, the more completely that person will see Christ.

One reason why traditional one-to-one evangelism may sometimes be unfruitful is that the non-Christian looks at a Christian and says, "Well, if that's what a Christian is, I certainly don't want to be one." Perhaps that Christian person is the only picture the non-Christian has ever had of the varied changes and spiritual fruit Christ produces in the lives of Christians.

Unfortunately, for many church members when it comes to exemplifying Christ in their lives, well . . . they come across as being only too human. "Dull of hearing" and "unskilled in the word of righteousness" (Heb. 5:11, 13 NKJV) is the way the Bible puts it. While a Christian is a new creature in the sense that Christ is the new center of his or her being, he or she still carries many imperfections. Often the imperfections in the Christian's life are the part that a non-Christian sees, and on that basis the non-Christian rejects the invitation to the Christian life. Therefore, in our desire to portray the love of Christ, the greater number of experiences a non-Christian has with the variety of members that make up the body of Christ, the more likely he or she is to see through the human shortcomings of individual Christians and perceive the wholeness that Jesus Christ brings to his people.

A third reason why a team effort is more productive in disciple making within one's oikos is that on a practical level, these non-Christians have to make new Christian friends in the church or they won't stay! Research indicates that in most cases people who make a decision for Christ and then drop out of church involvement never make new friends in that church. Evangelism that does not include this important "friendship factor" will result in much loss of labor. Disciple making is most effective when it is a team effort.

Principle 6

Disciple making is most effective when it is church centered.

The more distant evangelism is from the local church, the less fruit that remains; the closer evangelism is to the local church, the more fruit that remains. An effective strategy for disciple making revolves around the local church. It is energized through the local church. The results accrue to the local church. The process of disciple making has the church at the center of the evangelistic focus and builds on the vast resources available through the body.

What does "church-centered disciple making" mean?

While the church's unique role in The Master's Plan is examined in detail in chapters 6 and 7, the following functions of the church are central to effective disciple making:

- The church initiates disciple making through an intentional strategy.

- The church trains its members in effective disciple making.
- The church coordinates the resources of the body for effective disciple making.

Show Them the Whole Picture

Often if evangelism is ineffective in making new disciples, the problem can be traced to the method of presentation. Non-Christians need an opportunity to accurately perceive and understand God's love and grace as seen through the larger body of Christ. Effective disciple making should introduce unchurched friends and relatives to the variety of ways God works in people. The insightful children's poem "The Blind Men and the Elephant" is an excellent analogy of the need to help non-Christians experience the totality of Christ's love through the body.

The Blind Men and the Elephant
by John Godfrey Saxe

It was six men of Indostan
To learning much inclined,
Who went to see the elephant
(Though all of them were blind),
That each by observation
Might satisfy his mind.

The First approached the elephant,
And happening to fall
Against his broad and sturdy side,
At once began to bawl:
"God bless me! but the elephant
Is nothing but a wall."

The Second, feeling of the tusk,
Cried, "Ho! what have we here
So very round and smooth and sharp?
To me 'tis mighty clear
This wonder of an elephant
Is very like a spear!"

The Third approached the animal,
And, happening to take
The squirming trunk within his hands,
Thus boldly up and spake,
"I see," quoth he, "the elephant is very like a snake!"

The Fourth reached out his eager hand
And felt about the knee:
"What most this wondrous beast is like
Is mighty plain," quoth he:
"'Tis clear enough the elephant
Is very like a tree!"

The Fifth who chanced to touch the ear,
Said, "E'en the blindest man
Can tell what this resembles most;
Deny the fact who can,
This marvel of an elephant,
Is very like a fan!"

The Sixth no sooner had begun
About the beast to grope,
Than, seizing on the swinging tail
That fell within his scope,
"I see," quoth he, "the elephant
Is very like a rope!"

And so these men of Indostan
Disputed loud and long,
Each in his own opinion
Exceeding stiff and strong,
Though each was partly in the right,
All were in the wrong![2]

- The church creates programs and ministries for effective disciple making.
- The church structures accountability into disciple making.
- The church incorporates new disciples into the body.

Principle 7

Disciple making is most effective when unique needs and individual differences are recognized and celebrated.

"I have, in short, been all things to all sorts of men, that by every possible means I might win some to God. I do this all for the sake of the Gospel" (1 Cor. 9:22–23 PHILLIPS).

A barrier that often stops many people from becoming Christians is one we create ourselves. It grows out of the assumption that all people come to Christ in the same way, that they all have the same needs and the same problems, and that our simple memorized steps to eliciting a Christian decision will respond to their need.

The fact is that people come to Christ in many different ways, for many different reasons. And for Christ to be considered as a viable alternative in anyone's life, the gospel must be presented in ways that speak to those unique needs.

Effective disciple making recognizes the unique differences of the non-Christian friends and relatives in each member's web. The way God's love is communicated is based on an understanding of these differences. The following questions help clarify some of them.

- What is the level and depth of my relationship with this person?
- What other Christians does he or she know well?
- What is his or her understanding of Christianity? What are his or her misunderstandings?

Why Do People Join the Church?

Different people join the church for different reasons. In an exploratory study, Edward A. Rauff, director of the Research and Information Center for the Lutheran Council in the U.S.A., asked 180 people to respond to the question, Why did you join the church?[3] Their answers fell into the following categories (some interviewees indicated more than one reason for their decision).

Family Relationships and Responsibilities

The dominant reason thirty respondents gave for establishing a relationship with a church was to keep the family together and to strengthen family life. The pull of a family member made them look toward the church.

The Influence of Christian People

Twenty-two respondents said they saw a difference in the quality of life of a friend, relative, neighbor, or coworker and then connected that difference in some way to the person's religious conviction or church membership.

A Church Visit, Program, Special Event, Sacred Act

Nineteen respondents recalled that when they visited a church for special occasions or were brought into some church programs, they felt called to a deeper awareness, reflection, or self-examination.

A Search for Community

A friendly atmosphere made eighteen respondents feel at home when they visited a church. It bespoke a relationship that was warmer and deeper than they had experienced in nonchurch groups. This warm welcome made a return easier.

A Personal Crisis

Seventeen respondents felt they had lost control of their lives. Various events prompted a reordering of priorities and values and a reaching out to the church for help in meeting needs not previously experienced.

The End of Rebellion

Fifteen respondents said their decision to join a church was made in response to a need to take up a role that had been laid aside, a need to "go home" and return to former values and principles.

The Influence of Pastors

The clergy were crucial in drawing twelve respondents into a congregational relationship. The one-on-one interactions with clergy were milestones in the spiritual journeys that ended in church affiliation.

God's Intervention

Twelve respondents described their turning toward the church as so sudden and unexpected and difficult to explain that it was "out of the blue," an act of God. God's divine intervention was also seen as a time of fulfillment after earlier starts toward some church relationship.

The Journey toward Truth

Eleven respondents pursued a personal and determined journey toward truth, often in the face of resistance. Square one in some journeys was a college course in intellectual history or the chance reading of some Christian author or an intense discussion with some Christian apologist.

A Feeling of Emptiness

Eleven respondents noted a "feeling of emptiness" although they had "everything." An aching, long-festering sense of hurt, or sudden discovery of great loneliness, nudged them along their way toward the church.

The Response to Evangelism

Ten respondents felt they had been reached through the formal efforts of a congregation that initiated an evangelism thrust within the community. They cited the gentle yet persistent concern of Christians as the reason for their church affiliation.

The Reaction to Guilt and Fear

Ten respondents gave intense testimony that joining the church freed them from a feeling of guilt and insecurity and gave them an assurance of salvation.

- How receptive is the person to becoming a Christian?
- Would this person feel comfortable in my church (regarding such factors as age, marital status, ethnicity, socioeconomic status, common interests)?
- Can my church meet the needs of this person?

An understanding of the unique qualities and needs of each member implies a unique approach in the disciple-making process, an approach that will vary from one person to another. While steps for reaching individual web members will be discussed in detail later, an important insight into effective disciple making is that memorized lines will not suit every person in every situation. A study of the gospel reveals that Christ himself gave a powerful demonstration of meeting people where they were, addressing the unique needs of each person, and presenting the gospel in a relevant and meaningful way. Compared with strangers, church members involved in reaching their web are better able to understand the individuality of each person, the needs he or she may have, and the appropriate ways to introduce the need-meeting alternative of Jesus Christ and his church.

Principle 8

Disciple making is most effective when biblical insights and church growth research are integrated.

Christ's parable of the talents provides one of many insights into his desire to see the church grow. In this parable the master was pleased with the servant who was given five talents and doubled his investment to ten. The master was equally pleased with the servant who doubled his two talents to four. To these two servants his reward was generous: "Well done, thou good and faithful servant" (Matt. 25:21, 23). But to the servant who had been given one talent and had buried it until the master returned, the rebuke was strong: "Throw this useless servant into the darkness outside, where he can weep and wail over his stupidity" (Matt. 25:30 PHILLIPS). The master expected and desired his servants to multiply the treasure he had left with them!

Church growth is a field of study that searches for answers to the questions of how a local church can effectively multiply its "talents" to result in new Christians and responsible church members. The principles of church growth are bringing renewed hope to churches concerned with reaching greater possibilities of ministry, outreach, and growth. Church growth principles are being successfully applied in churches across the country. Churches participating in The Master's Plan are using a process built on solid biblical and theological concepts as well as on the insights of years of church growth research.

Church growth principles can help make disciple making more effective in many ways. Did you know, for example, that church growth research has found that people in your web will vary over time as to their receptivity to the gospel? Did you know it is possible to tell when they are most receptive to becoming new disciples? Or did you know that the way a church member views the process of verbally sharing the gospel has an important effect on whether the non-Christian responds? Did you know that the events in the first few months of a new Christian's life often determine whether that person will continue as an active member or lose interest and drop out?

There are many important new insights into how people come to Christ and the church that creatively and consistently support the examples of Jesus and the early Christians and provide us with a practical process to see the Great Commission come alive in our congregation and community.

Principle 9

Disciple making is most effective as a natural and continuing process.

Continuous disciple making requires prudent stewardship of church members' time and energy. It requires an evangelistic process that renews rather than exhausts laity. It requires a process that is a natural part of life rather than a contrived event. This sounds like a tall order for pastors and those faithful in evangelism who may have struggled for years to enlist volunteers in calling programs or evangelism training events.

When does disciple making become a natural part of the Christian life?

1. When it builds on natural human relationships. A recent national survey asked the question, "What do you enjoy doing most in your spare time?" The answer, from 74 percent of the people surveyed, was, "Spending time with family and friends."[4]

God made people to enjoy other people. He made the family and the relationships that result. In every human culture on earth the family (or extended family) is the basic organizational structure.[5] God uses this natural network of family and friends to most effectively spread the Good News. The Master's Plan builds on this foundation.

2. When it builds on the need to love and be loved. People, both Christians and non-Christians, need caring and love. The Master's Plan responds to this need in the lives of church members and of the people in their web of influence. In the disciple-making process, Christians learn how to strengthen relationships with non-Christians and communicate God's caring through their own caring. "You shall love your neighbor as yourself" (Gal. 5:14). The commission of Christ is to share his love and to make disciples.

3. When it becomes part of the church's organizational structure. Effective, continuous disciple making does not translate into a program to be adopted, organized, and carried out by a few select members of an evangelism committee or calling team. It is a process that becomes a natural part of each organization in the church body. The women's circle, the Sunday school classes, the choir, the home Bible studies, are all able to become involved in the disciple-making process. Ideally, if a church member is involved in any church activity, he or she will be confronted with and encouraged in the opportunity to make disciples in that particular context.

4. When it is self-perpetuating. Effective disciple making can't help but be self-perpetuating. Indeed, not only does it continue but the process naturally enlarges. It happens when one person in a member's web comes to Christ and the body and then has his or her own web of relationships with friends and relatives outside Christ. As the new Christian identifies those people and begins making disciples, the growth and outreach process through the church enlarges again and again.

4

Seven Steps for Making Disciples

Pastor Austin and Chuck had just finished lunch together. As they returned to the church and were walking back to the church office, Pastor Austin asked, "Chuck, are you witnessing to anyone presently?"

Chuck was not proud of his answer. "No, not really."

There was a pause in the conversation as the two entered the pastor's study and sat down. "Is that because the people you relate to—your neighbors, your relatives, people you work with—are already believers?"

"Oh, no," answered Chuck. "I don't think any of the people I work with are believers. Neither are my neighbors. And relatives—well, maybe half are Christians."

"And with how many of these unreached people do you have a fairly close relationship?" asked Pastor Austin.

"Well, I guess I'm on a first-name basis or better with about nine or ten."

"So how are they responding to your witness?" asked the pastor.

At first Chuck thought he had heard wrong. "Responding? Didn't you hear what I said? I'm not witnessing to anyone."

Pastor Austin's words were disturbing: "Oh, but you are. Even if it's not intentional."

"You mean . . . the way I act? The things I say? The things I do? That's all part of my witness?"

Pastor Austin nodded.

Every day each of us comes into contact with unreached people with whom we have ongoing, established relationships. These people are called our "Extended Family."

Extended Family

If you are a father or mother, you no doubt feel an important sense of responsibility for your family. God has given you the duty to oversee their physical health, safety, personal growth, spiritual development.

But did you realize that God has given you an Extended Family for whom you also have a responsibility? They are members of your oikos—your close friends, your relatives, and your associates—who do not know Jesus Christ. The people in your Extended Family are those non-Christians with whom you have a unique relationship. In many cases you may be the only bridge God has to them.

Extended Family: A church member's close friends, relatives, and associates who are not in Christ and the church.

To develop your vocabulary in The Master's Plan, it is helpful to understand the difference between two terms: oikos and Extended Family.

Your oikos is composed of the people in your circle of influence—both Christians and non-Christians.

Your Extended Family, on the other hand, are the people in your oikos who are not in Christ and the church.

Chuck considered his own Extended Family—those people he knew who were not Christians.

There was Jim, the art director at Chuck's office; Chuck's younger sister, Mary, who was getting a divorce; Pete, Chuck's next-door neighbor; Fred, a friend at the gym where Chuck worked out twice a week; and Chuck's cousin, Sue, who lived a few miles away. Chuck saw each of these people frequently and shared with them a relationship based on mutual respect. Yet none were Christians.

So how do you begin such a significant adventure as seeing those in your Extended Family come to Christ and the church? Here are seven important steps.

Step 1. Identify Your Extended Family

Analyze the regular contacts you have with people in your day-to-day life. Consider the people in each of the following groups: kin, friends, and associates.

Those people who are related to you biologically or through marriage constitute the kinship area of your Extended Family. One person's immediate family may be composed of a spouse and children. For another, it may include parents, brothers, or sisters. Other family members, such as cousins, aunts, uncles, in-laws, nieces, nephews, and grandparents, may be part of an Extended Family.

Close friends are also part of your Extended Family. Through friendship you can identify people whom you regard as confidants—those you trust, those with whom you share plans and experiences, joys and sorrows. These are friends with whom you regularly communicate in person or by phone. Neighbors whom you know on a first-name basis are part of your Extended Family. Those you invite over for a backyard barbecue or social event, those you look forward to being with, are all part of the common friendship segment of your Extended Family.

The associates area of your Extended Family may include people at work or school with whom you rub shoulders daily. Perhaps you enjoy coffee or lunch together. You share family news, talk about current events, and discuss matters of mutual interest pertaining to your work. Maybe you participate in sports or other recreational activities together. Also in the associates part of your Extended Family may be people with whom you perform civic work or are involved in special clubs or projects. Perhaps you solicit funds together or work on a committee or share a mutual concern for your city and its quality of life.

Identifying and listing those six, eight, or ten people who compose your Extended Family is an important first step in seeing them come to Christ and the church.

Step 2. Develop a Profile of Each Member

Franklin D. Roosevelt made it a point to become a friend to every dignitary he met. Before a foreign leader came to visit, the president would study the person's hobbies, special interests, and areas of personal concern. When the diplomat and the president met, they first talked on an official, political level. But then the conversation often changed. The president would praise the diplomat for any special achievements he had made, direct the discussion to the diplomat's hobbies or interests, and listen attentively as he spoke. Through expressions of genuine interest, Roosevelt built friendships that endured a lifetime.

Knowing a person on a level beyond biographical details of age, marital status, and occupation is part of effective disciple making. The more we understand the interests, concerns, and needs of our Extended Family members, the deeper and more substantial our relationships with them will be.

What do you know about the members of your Extended Family? What are their backgrounds? What do they do in their spare time? What are their attitudes toward various subjects? How are their family lives, and what concerns do they have in that area? Are they happy in their jobs? What important events are they experiencing in their lives?

What do you know about the spiritual lives of the members in your Extended Family? What are their previous religious experiences? What knowledge do they have about the Bible? What do they understand or misunderstand about the Christian life? What attitudes do they display concerning "Christian things"? Are they open or antagonistic about discussing spiritual matters? Do they have any Christian friends?

Also, note why you think the person is not a believer. Has he or she heard the gospel, been invited to accept Christ, perceived no need for a relationship with Christ, chosen another religious lifestyle?

You may not know the answer to all these questions. If not, this is an important place to begin the disciple-making process—simply getting to know the person in a more meaningful way.

Step 3. Focus Your Efforts

As you review the list of names in your Extended Family, you may want to identify several people with whom you have a natural, warm relationship. They are people with whom you get along well. You enjoy doing things together and have a variety of common interests. They may be people who would enjoy being with your friends from church. These people should be ones you feel are receptive to the gospel and could easily find a home in your congregation.

The number of people you can focus on may differ according to the amount of time you give to consciously sharing God's love. A busy executive, for example, may have time to work effectively with only one or two people at a time, whereas a retired person could easily focus on six or more non-Christians in his or her Extended Family.

Chuck identified three members of his Extended Family to focus on: Pete, his next-door neighbor, Mary, his sister, and Fred, his friend from the gym.

Pete was married but had no children. His wife was six months pregnant. Pete's favorite recreational pastime was fishing. He repeatedly invited Chuck to go, but so far Chuck had never accepted. Pete's church background was "zero."

Mary was getting a divorce after seven years of marriage. They had no children, and she was twenty-eight years old. At one time Mary was active in church, but after her marriage to a non-Christian she became inactive. Mary was currently unemployed and had a high school education. She worked a few years prior to her marriage but had acquired no marketable skill.

As for Fred, Chuck saw him regularly down at the gym where they both worked out twice a week. They enjoyed sharing information about their respective families, jobs, and the weather but never saw each other outside the gym.

Step 4. Develop a Disciple-Making Plan

Scripture's admonition to plan carefully is particularly applicable to making disciples: "Any enterprise is built by wise planning, becomes strong through common sense, and profits wonderfully by keeping abreast of the facts" (Prov. 24:3–4 TLB).

Introducing non-Christian friends and relatives to Christ and directing their attention to the opportunity of new life demands our best efforts. Yet often we tend to run ahead in our evangelistic methods without first considering insights that might increase our effectiveness.

Our disciple-making plans must begin with meeting people at their point of need. Paul said, "I have become all things to all people, that I may by all means save some" (1 Cor. 9:22). Effective plans for communicating the gospel must recognize the unique ways hearers perceive the Good News and relate it to their lives and needs.

Christ's approach to introducing the kingdom to people was highly individualistic. It was often based on events with which the listener could readily identify. He met people on their own ground. He respected them as individuals with unique interests and needs. He asked the woman at the well for a drink of water. He told stories about sowing and harvesting to people who understood such things.

Because the disciple-making plan you develop for your Extended Family members is so important, the next chapter is devoted to making an effective plan.

Step 5. Work the Disciple-Making Plan

As you begin to implement the steps of your disciple-making plan, be sensitive to and aware of the events in your Extended Family member's life. There could be a right time and a wrong time, a right way and a wrong way, to communicate Christ's love.

Here are some suggestions for developing skills in effective communication with Extended Family members.

A. Listen Attentively

Paul Tillich, a prominent theologian, once said, "The first duty of love is to listen."[1] Almost everyone is born with the capacity to hear. However, the ability to listen must be learned and cultivated through practice. Attentive listening is a valuable skill for every layperson concerned with effective disciple making.

Chuck had been trying to really listen to his friend Fred's ideas and opinions. Chuck found listening to be hard work, since he enjoyed talking, even to the point of monopolizing many conversations. But as he and Fred worked out in the gym, Chuck was beginning to listen. The result was a deepening of their friendship as Fred began sharing more of himself with Chuck.

What is attentive listening? It is concentrating on what the other person is saying, rather than letting our mind race ahead to what should be said next. It is putting ourselves in the other person's shoes. It is seeing things from his or her perspective rather than our own. It is empathetic, comprehending, and nonjudgmental.

Another element of attentive listening is body language—eye contact, an encouraging nod, an understanding smile. A study in communication effectiveness showed that words alone carry only about 7 percent of the message. The tone of delivery contributes 33 percent. Yet the nonverbal aspect—the body language—communicates 55 percent of the message.

Attentive listening has no hidden agenda. It is not geared toward turning the conversation to spiritual matters at the first opportunity. Rather, it seeks to understand the non-Christian friend's dreams and ambitions, to discover his or her needs and problems, and to develop a level of understanding that builds a mutual respect and personal empathy.

B. Relate to Needs

God's love is the greatest need-meeting resource on earth. Be alert to the unique needs of your Extended Family members.

A close and meaningful relationship includes mutual sharing of experiences—happiness, sadness, success, failure, irritation, disappointment. It is in the personal experiences of life that the importance of faith and fellowship in the church often become apparent. Areas of need in your life or in the lives of your Extended Family members provide a natural context for demonstrating your Christian faith, relating your experiences to theirs, and discussing the solution Christ has provided you. "I shall make mention of the lovingkindness of the LORD, the praises of the LORD, according to all that the LORD has granted us" (Isa. 63:7).

Following their workout, Chuck and Fred were talking in the gym dressing room. The conversation turned toward their families, and Fred began to talk about his daughter. "Tina's mixed up with kids that Joan and I think are headed for trouble, and she just won't listen to us. Frankly, we don't know what to do or where to turn."

"That can be pretty tough," said Chuck sympathetically. "Peer pressure can really be powerful. We had similar problems with Karen."

"What did you do about it?" asked Fred.

"Well, we've tried to let Karen know that we love her and that God loves her. I also think that becoming more involved in the youth group at our church has been a big help."

Chuck went on to describe briefly the family counseling program available through his church.

The next day Fred checked out the church's counseling program and soon he, his wife, and their daughter were involved—all because Chuck had been able to honestly identify with Fred at his point of need.

C. Identify Receptive Periods

God's love and caring are especially appropriate during significant changes in lifestyle (such as marriage, birth of a child, new job, retirement) or incidents of stress (death of a spouse, divorce, family crisis, injury) in our Extended Family members' lives. These times are called periods of transition. A period of transition is a span of time in which a person's or family's normal, everyday behavior patterns are disrupted by some event that puts them into an unfamiliar situation. The more recent the event in the person's life, the more receptive he or she will be to a new lifestyle that includes Christ and the church. Consequently, it is important to stay in close touch with your Extended Family members and respond immediately in a time of transition. Being aware of these periods of transition in our non-Christian friends and responding by showing them the caring love of Christ and the church can be an important step in seeing them become new disciples.

The antithesis of this receptivity principle is also a factor in your disciple-making activities. That is, an Extended Family member in a stable situation, with few complications or unusual interruptions in his or her life, is generally not as open to becoming a disciple. Often the only way to reach an Extended Family member not open to the Christian faith is to be alert to a period of transition, when his or her receptivity will increase, and then respond in love by sharing Christ's love.

D. Use Appropriate Timing

When you communicate God's love and the Christian experience can be as important as *what* you communicate. The most effective witness comes at the appropri-

Receptivity Scale

Figure 2 indicates different events, in approximate order of their importance, that have an effect in producing periods of personal or family transition.[2] The numbers on the left indicate the importance of the event relative to other transition-producing events. Various events may compound each other when an individual experiences more than one incident over a relatively short period of time. The higher the number, the more receptive the person is to the gospel. For example, someone who was just married and is also having trouble with his or her boss will be more receptive than if either event had occurred separately. Also, the larger the number or accumulation of numbers, the longer the period of transition will last and the more intense it will be.

ate moment. For example, when Fred explained his difficulty with his daughter to Chuck in the gym, it was an appropriate moment for Chuck to relate how his faith guided him in similar circumstances. The timing was ideal for Chuck to communicate the church's support and suggest a Christian answer to an important question Fred was facing.

E. Use Understandable Language

Sharing the realities and benefits of Christ in everyday language, in the context of your everyday experience, gives a credibility and relevance to the Christian faith that is critical to an Extended Family member. As you mention your faith and the difference in your life because of it, speak in words and phrases the person will understand. Sharing your experience helps your non-Christian friend or relative sense that your relationship with Christ has an

Figure 2

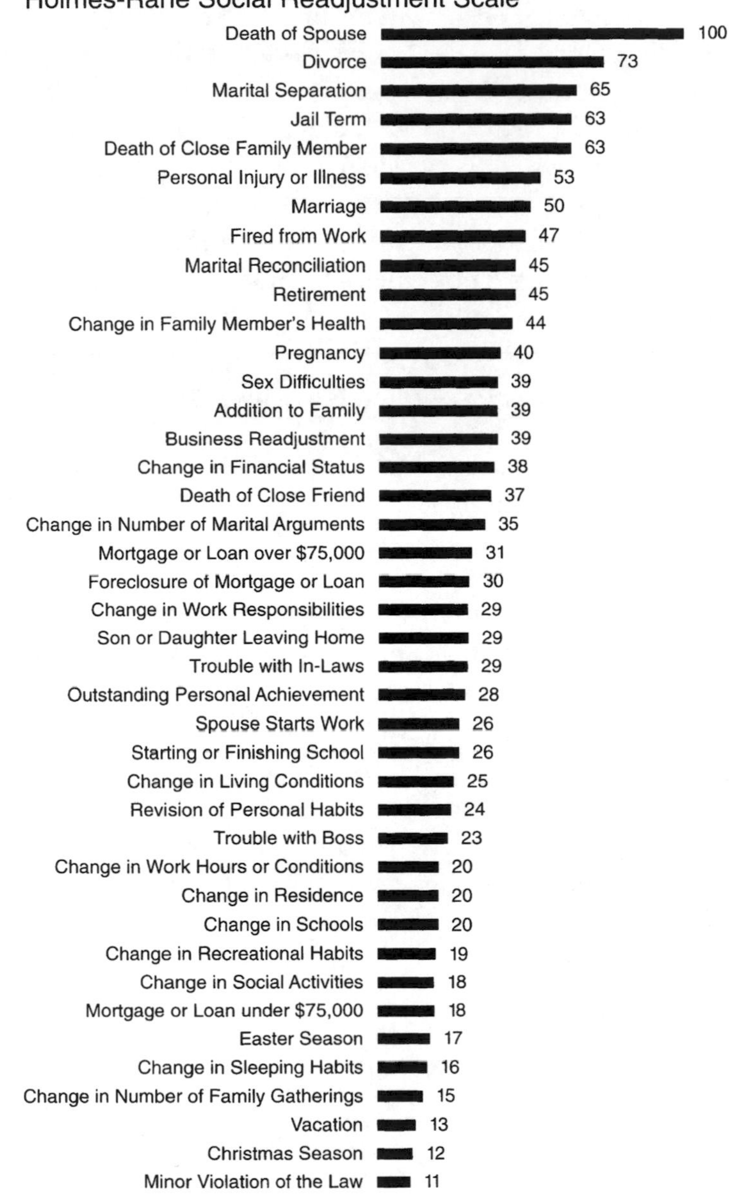
Holmes-Rahe Social Readjustment Scale
Death of Spouse 100
Divorce 73
Marital Separation 65
Jail Term 63
Death of Close Family Member 63
Personal Injury or Illness 53
Marriage 50
Fired from Work 47
Marital Reconciliation 45
Retirement 45
Change in Family Member's Health 44
Pregnancy 40
Sex Difficulties 39
Addition to Family 39
Business Readjustment 39
Change in Financial Status 38
Death of Close Friend 37
Change in Number of Marital Arguments 35
Mortgage or Loan over $75,000 31
Foreclosure of Mortgage or Loan 30
Change in Work Responsibilities 29
Son or Daughter Leaving Home 29
Trouble with In-Laws 29
Outstanding Personal Achievement 28
Spouse Starts Work 26
Starting or Finishing School 26
Change in Living Conditions 25
Revision of Personal Habits 24
Trouble with Boss 23
Change in Work Hours or Conditions 20
Change in Residence 20
Change in Schools 20
Change in Recreational Habits 19
Change in Social Activities 18
Mortgage or Loan under $75,000 18
Easter Season 17
Change in Sleeping Habits 16
Change in Number of Family Gatherings 15
Vacation 13
Christmas Season 12
Minor Violation of the Law 11

important influence on your attitudes and actions in everyday circumstances. Paul told the Christians at Colossae, "Make the most of your chances to tell others the Good News. Be wise in all your contacts with them. Let your conversation be gracious as well as sensible, for then you will have the right answer for everyone" (Col. 4:5–6 TLB).

Each of the above suggestions will help you understand and respond more effectively to the unique concerns of your Extended Family member.

Step 6. Pray Regularly for Each Member

"The earnest prayer of a righteous man has great power and wonderful results" (James 5:16 TLB).

Prayer must be at the very heart of the disciple-making process. The importance of regular prayer for members of your Extended Family cannot be overemphasized. If this vital step is overlooked, the chances of ever seeing your Extended Family member come to Christ and the church are slim. "When you want to reach someone for Christ, begin with the least intimidating approach—prayer."[3]

After you have identified the people in your Extended Family, pray daily for each of them and for their needs. Do you remember the definition of caring? "Allowing God's love to flow through you to people, especially those in your network of relationships." Ask God to let your Extended Family members experience his love through you.

In prayer we express our concerns for each person in our Extended Family. We should pray according to their unique needs, attitudes, and situations. It may well be that a person in our Extended Family has never before been held up to God in prayer. What a thrill to be the first one to have that privilege! And it is impossible to talk daily with the Lord about a person and not become genuinely concerned about the person and aware of caring and sharing opportunities you have with him or her.

One of the most important activities of a church committed to helping members disciple their Extended Families is regular prayer offered by members for the non-Christians in each other's oikos. Wayne McDill has correctly observed that "greater strength can be brought to bear in your prayers as you involve others in praying for your friend."[4] Jesus provided a promise at this very point: "If two of you agree on earth about anything that they may ask, it shall be done for them by My Father who is in heaven" (Matt. 18:19).

Each layperson involved in making disciples should pray not only for the non-Christians in his or her web but for people in other members' Extended Families. Sharing prayer concerns, asking God for a sense of awareness to opportunities that arise, and thanking him for answered prayer are important parts of each person's role in making disciples.

Step 7. Accept Accountability to Others and to God

Meet regularly with other Christians involved in the disciple-making process. As you discuss goals and individual experiences, you will find an important sense of support, fellowship, and accountability.

No two Christians' caring relationships with Extended Family members will be identical. Thus, sharing individual successes and failures can provide rich learning experiences for every church member involved. One person's insights sharpen another's understanding. And the probability of each member continuing as a disciple maker is increased when he or she is part of a group that meets regularly.

In these times, members share their concerns for each person in their Extended Families. These concerns become the subject of intercessory prayer for the entire group. Likewise, experiences of answered prayer are shared with the group and expressed in praise and thanks to the Lord.

Praying for fellow church members is an encouraging and enabling aspect of these times together. Thanking God for the opportunity to demonstrate his love and Word through a caring witness helps members keep their disciple-making ministry at the forefront of their Christian lives. As Christians ask God for guidance, wisdom, insight, and sensitivity, they build a confidence and self-worth in being ambassadors of God's love. These times of prayer together are a mutual expression of dependence, anticipation, and assurance of God's ability to direct his people.

Church members may want to become prayer partners with one another. Each agrees to pray for his or her partner and the members of that person's Extended Family. The disciple-making process is strengthened immeasurably as each Extended Family member is daily held up by others before the Lord in prayer.

Your Opportunity

Is it possible to see the lives of friends, relatives, and associates really change as they encounter the miraculous love of Christ? Can you, as an "ordinary layperson," have a meaningful and purposeful role in reaching these people with Christ's love? The answer is a resounding, affirmative yes! You can do it! In fact, you are probably the person best able to show these Extended Family members the burden-lifting power of Jesus Christ.

5 How to Reach Your Extended Family

It was late afternoon, and Diane had invited her friend Judy for a quick cup of coffee. This had become a regular ritual since Judy returned to work. Judy was recently divorced and was the mother of three small children. She was working again, not because she wanted to, but because she had to.

"Diane, it's so frustrating to work as a clerk-typist in the same office I once managed."

"That must be hard," replied Diane sympathetically.

"And all because I took ten years out of my life to try to start a family." Judy brought her cup to the kitchen sink. "Well, enough of this crying on your shoulder. I've got to pick the kids up from the sitter. Thanks for the coffee."

"You're welcome. Maybe next week we could get together for lunch."

"I'd like that."

After Judy left, Diane breathed a silent prayer for her divorced friend. She asked particularly for wisdom in knowing the best ways to show Judy that God loved her.

You will remember that in the steps to disciple making we discussed in the previous chapter, step 4 was to develop a disciple-making plan for the members of your Extended Family.

One of the most important steps in reaching friends and relatives in your Extended Family is devising an appropriate and effective strategy for introducing those people to Christ and his body. Here are some key insights that will help you come up with an effective plan to communicate God's love to each person in your Extended Family.

Caring

Your most important role as a witness to the people in your Extended Family is personifying Christ's love. Christ's love is communicated through your caring.

Here is a principle of effective disciple making: "God's love is best seen and experienced by others through our love."

Consider the implications of this concept! The traditional requirements of a good witness (that is, verbal fluency, extrovert personality, tenacity) become less important than simply being an open channel through which God's love can be seen and experienced by those in your Extended Family. Think of it—you become the channel for God's love! Exciting? Yes! Possible? Absolutely!

God's great love for these potential disciples, and his desire to express that love, is seen throughout Scripture. As he first loved us, we express our love for him through loving others: "'For I was hungry and you fed me; I was thirsty and you gave me water; I was a stranger and you invited me into your homes; naked and you clothed me; sick and in prison, and you visited me.' Then these righteous ones will reply, 'Sir, when did we ever see you hungry and feed you? Or thirsty and give you anything to drink? Or a stranger, and help you? Or naked, and clothe you? When did we ever see you sick or in prison, and visit you?' And I, the King, will tell them, 'When you did it to these my brothers you were doing it to me!'" (Matt. 25:35–40 TLB).

Scripture illustrates what love for Christ entails. It is a basic, down-to-earth involvement with people in need. The response is to be personal and caring. The people in your Extended Family may not require clothing, food, or water. But they do have real needs. Responding to the void of loneliness, frustration, or despair demands a personal investment of genuine caring.

David Augsburger, in his book *Caring Enough to Confront,* observes that caring people "dare to be present with people . . . and to stand with people where they are hurting. . . . Caring people look for the opportunity of affirming, of encouraging, of helping release others to become all they can be in Christ."[1] Caring for the members of your Extended Family is an ongoing process. Does one meal satisfy a hungry person for life? Does one visit to a lonely person cause his or her loneliness to disappear? Caring requires an investment of time and patience. Paul Cedar notes, "You simply cannot love another only on your schedule. You must be willing to be available when the other person needs you. Availability is an essential ingredient of authentic love."[2]

Here is a helpful way of understanding Christ's perfect love: by substituting the name *Jesus* for the word *love* in Paul's great chapter 13 of 1 Corinthians. "Jesus was patient, kind, never jealous, boastful or arrogant. He did not act unbecomingly, did not first seek His own interests, was not touchy; did not keep account of wrongs suffered nor gloat over the hardships of others. His greatest joy was seeing truth come to life. He accepted all that people said or did to Him, trusted all who approached Him, believed the best for all who despaired. He set no limits for what He could endure. His concern, respect, and compassion could outlast anything."[3] Christ is a model for our caring relationships with Extended Family members. The caring aspect of making disciples reflects God's very nature: "God is love" (1 John 4:8).

Diane and Judy were sitting in the kitchen of the Bradley home one afternoon, having another cup of coffee.

"Without your help and friendship, Diane, I don't think I could have survived these last three months. When Tom walked out on me, I was devastated," said Judy.

"Isn't that what friends are for . . . to help each other?"

"I guess . . ." Judy replied. "But no one's ever been this kind to me before, not even my own family." After a pause she continued, "Diane, do you really like me . . . as a person?"

"You know I do," Diane replied.

"Yes, but I also know that you've got some kind of religious faith, even though you've never talked much about it. You go to church on Sundays. You've got Bibles and religious books lying around. I've got to know. Are you being nice to me because you're trying to convert me?"

Diane was somewhat taken aback by the question. "Judy, my friendship is not some kind of bait to get you to join my church or become a Christian. But my faith does have something to do with my caring for you."

"I knew it," said Judy. "You have got an angle."

"Please hear me out," said Diane earnestly. "My faith isn't just in a religion, it's in a person—Jesus Christ. And he has radically changed my life. There was a time when I could never love someone without, as you call it, an angle. But because of Jesus Christ in my life, I'm beginning to."

"Does that mean you'll still be my friend, even if I don't want your religion?"

"Yes, of course I will."

Diane was exemplifying an important insight: Our caring and friendship with others must be unconditional. It is not the bait of a religious trap, nor is it the means to an end. Unconditional caring is a reflection of God's unswerving and unrelenting love. If a friend were to say, "I don't want anything to do with your religion," should your caring be any less than before? Do you think God's love is any less for those who reject him? If anything, God's concern is even greater. How many people have once rejected his love and then later, perhaps in a time of need, responded and are now active, reproducing Christians? Caring must be genuine and unconditional and not depend on how a person responds to spiritual overtures.

"Unfortunately," observes Paul Little, in his book *How to Give Away Your Faith*, "many non-Christians today are suspicious of all Christians because of a previous contact with a 'friendly' religious person who had ulterior motives. Some non-Christians refuse to listen to a single word about our Lord until they're sure we'll be their friends, even if they reject Jesus Christ. We must love each person for him/herself."[4] Christ wants his lost children found. We should not take it upon ourselves to close the door on the relationship that God has (through us) with these Extended Family members. Caring must be genuine, long term, and unconditional.

Strengthening Relationships

Your disciple-making effectiveness is enhanced where strong relationships exist with members of your Extended

Family. The apostle John writes, "Dear friends, let us practice loving each other, for love comes from God and those who are loving and kind show that they are the children of God" (1 John 4:7 TLB).

What person does not enjoy the companionship of a loving, caring friend! A strong and growing relationship between you and your Extended Family member contributes immeasurably to allowing the Holy Spirit to speak to that person.

In *The Friendship Factor* Alan McGinnis says, "It is no accident so many important encounters occurred between Jesus and His friends when they were at the table. There is something almost sacramental about breaking bread with one another."[5] Invite your friend to attend a special event that you both will enjoy. Drop by his or her home with something from your garden, workshop, or flower bed. Perhaps you could make it a point to have coffee or lunch once a week with the person in your Extended Family.

Do you know of any special needs your friend has that could be a point of relationship building? For example, does he or she need help laying a brick walk, hanging drapes, or painting the house? Strong friendships come with shared experiences. "Working shoulder to shoulder strengthens a relationship even when few words are spoken."[6]

As your relationship grows, expect your Extended Family member to also respond to your needs. Friendship is not a one-way affair. The close relationship will be as meaningful to you as to your Extended Family member. The joy and fulfillment that comes from being with friends and giving of yourself is one of the emotional highlights of life. Enjoy it!

Scripture speaks repeatedly of joy as an integral part of a relationship, both with the Lord and with one another. "If we are living in the light of God's presence, just as Christ does, then we have wonderful fellowship and joy with each other" (1 John 1:7 TLB). As you look through God's eyes at your Extended Family members—made in his image to be part of his family—take pleasure in loving those people and directing their attention toward God's love. Wayne McDill points out that "as an expression of our love for them, we endeavor to communicate the vast resources available through Christ and His Church, and what God can do to make life a meaningful and rewarding experience."[7] This selfless concern results in a unique sense of inner joy and fulfillment. Each of us has the privilege of being an ambassador of Jesus Christ and his love.

Here is an important distinction that should be pointed out: The idea of "friendship evangelism" is not new in evangelism circles. A number of programs have been built on an approach that encourages Christians to "make friends to win souls." It would be a mistake to interpret the emphasis of friendship and caring found throughout The Master's Plan to be one of manipulation or scheming to get a decision for Christ. There is a difference between the *reason* for a relationship (to get a convert) and the *result* of a caring relationship (often a new disciple). Build your friendship with sincerity and unconditional caring.

A helpful study shows the importance of friendship in the process of becoming a new disciple. The study, reported in *Church Growth: America* magazine, identified 240 new Christians active and involved in their churches. In addition, a second group of 240 people could be classified as "dropouts" (they had made a recent decision but had since lapsed into inactivity). A third group of 240 people had been presented with the gospel message but had chosen not to make a positive decision. In individual interviews with these 720 people, each was asked to put the person who had presented the gospel to them in one of three categories: "friend," "salesman," "teacher." The results provided some startling conclusions. Almost all the people who saw the church member as a friend were now Christians and active in their churches (94 percent). On the other hand, those people who saw the church member as a salesman often made an initial decision but soon dropped out in large numbers (71 percent later dropped out). Finally, those who saw the church member as a teacher generally tended not to respond at all (84 percent said no thanks).[8] The implications are clear. The non-Christian who perceives you as a friend is more likely to respond to Christ's love than the person who sees you either as a teacher (instructing him or her on doctrine, sin, and morality) or as a salesman (manipulating him or her toward a decision).

Your greatest resource in developing a meaningful and caring friendship is in simply being yourself—natural and unmasked. The phrase "I'm not perfect, just forgiven" reflects a healthy attitude in recognizing the shortcomings each person has. The unique benefit of the Christian life is in the strength and support from a source greater than ourselves. When your Extended Family member understands this simple truth, it may change his or her attitude toward faith and life in Christ.

As you spend time with your Extended Family members, your sense of values and purpose in life naturally surfaces. In his book *Power in Praise* Merlin Carothers observes that "if we grumble and complain as bitterly as our non-Christian friends over the many little upsetting incidents of the day, others conclude that our faith does no more than occupy an hour of our time Sunday morning."[9] How do you react to delays or difficulties on the job, to emergencies, to everyday encounters? Do you respond in a way that causes non-Christian friends and relatives to see a difference that suggests the quality of your life in Christ?

Diane discovered the insight of simply being yourself, following a stressful event in her life, an event that her friend Judy happened to witness. She and Judy were at the Bradley home when Diane's sister called with the tragic news that their parents had been in an automobile accident and their mother had been killed.

Judy watched as Diane sat down and started to cry. After a moment Judy asked, "Doesn't it help—I mean, your faith?"

"Sure, it helps," answered Diane. "I know I'll see Mom again. I have that hope. But being a Christian doesn't take away the pain."

Somehow Judy had assumed that Christians never experienced pain or grief. Sharing that time of sorrow with Diane was a turning point in Judy's life. Realizing that Christians are not isolated from reality was a big step forward in Judy's decision to become a disciple.

Using Other Members of the Body

To successfully communicate God's love to your Extended Family members, use the unique resource of your church. The local church is a central part of the disciple-making process. In fact, disciple making simply cannot be effective outside the context of the local church. One obvious reason is that the goal is to make disciples, and a disciple is one who is involved in and incorporated into the life of a local church—namely, yours.

One important disciple-making resource found in your church is other church members, particularly your close friends. Encouraging and building personal relationships between your Extended Family members and Christian friends in your church is an effective way of introducing your non-Christian friends to the variety of ways Christ works in the lives of people. No person other than Jesus has ever been a perfect example of the Christian life. If you are the only Christian your Extended Family member knows, his or her perception of the incarnation of Christ in a person's life is limited to what he or she sees in you.

What a unique new perspective to sharing God's love: introducing Christ to your Extended Family member through the people in your church. And how much more accurate an introduction than one simple explanation of who and what Christ is, from a single source.

This "cross-pollination" between your Extended Family members and various Christians in your church adds a dynamic dimension to the disciple-making process. It provides you, as a disciple maker, with support from other members, and in turn you become part of other church members' disciple-making activities as you build relationships with their Extended Family members. The process adds to the effectiveness of disciple making, to the common concern of church members for non-Christians, and to the accountability of church members regarding the people in their Extended Families. The process of communicating God's love through the lives of other Christians takes the burden of responsibility off the back of just one person. Christians can look to the body and its members for support in making disciples.

How do you help such relationships flourish between your Extended Family members and others in the congregation? Informal social gatherings at your home or group outings to special events can include both Christian and non-Christian friends. The church may want to sponsor a series of special events or workshops of interest to non-Christians. The purpose of the events would be to provide an opportunity for building relationships between Extended Family members and church members.

Christians introduced to other members' friends should make it a point to be as friendly and caring as they would hope other church members would be to their own unreached friends. An "Extended Family consciousness," which encourages church members to build warm and potentially ongoing relationships with non-Christians met through other church members, should begin to develop.

You may want to use church programs, classes, and activities to introduce your Extended Family to others in the church. A special, elective Sunday school class might be of interest to your friend, or perhaps a worship service in which a particular message would be relevant. Church-sponsored social events are excellent opportunities to bring a non-Christian friend and introduce him or her to friends in the church. Another approach could be to enlist your Extended Family members in an ongoing group, perhaps a home Bible study or a weekly lunch meeting, with some friends from church.

Chuck's neighbor Pete loved fishing. To strengthen their relationship, Chuck accepted Pete's invitation to go fishing. And the second time they went out, Chuck arranged for Andrew, a church member who loved fishing, to go as well.

As for Fred, his friend at the gym, Chuck arranged some bowling dates with him, inviting two men from the church to make up a foursome.

Chuck encouraged his sister Mary to attend a church-sponsored seminar on coping with divorce. Since Mary was in need of a job, Chuck introduced her to two young career women from the church who were now helping Mary study for her real estate license. The three women were becoming good friends.

Through these various contacts with the ministries and people from his church, three members of Chuck's Extended Family were learning more about Christ's love and how he is exemplified in the lives of others.

From the church perspective, providing opportunities for members to build relationships with the Extended Family members of others in the church is a major step in effective disciple making. Activities sponsored by the church for building such relationships may not directly present the gospel message, but they meet important needs and establish meaningful contacts that communicate the love of Christ to potential disciples. (Chapter 6 is devoted to the church's important role in disciple making.)

Enhancing Your Witness

As you plan how to communicate God's love to your Extended Family, the question, But what do I say? naturally arises. To find the answer to that question, let's turn to the Bible.

In searching Scripture to learn what to say, one is impressed that there is no one simple formula that was used. Every situation was different. Indeed, the Bible presents a variety of illustrations of how people came to faith. Noted scholar P. T. Forsyth has observed of the New Testament model, "There was no universal theological formula. There was not an orthodoxy, but certainly there was a common apostolic gospel, or kerygma."[10]

Jesus, in teaching his disciples to be fishers of men, used many different models, from Nicodemus, the religious ruler who was told he needed to be "born again" (John 3:3), to the woman of Samaria who was offered water of eternal life (John 4:14), to the thief on the cross who asked only to be remembered when Christ came into his kingdom (Luke

23:42). Each situation presented different needs, portrayed different relationships, used different words, brought a different response. Each situation was unique.

However, while there was no one formula, there were common denominators of the gospel presentations that appeared again and again in biblical models. What are they?

Features of Gospel Presentations in the Bible

The Assumption: Humanity's Sinful Nature

The teachings of Jesus, the apostles, and the early church all assume the common sinfulness of humankind. Because of humanity's sinful nature, the gospel embodies a call to repentance and faith. Scripture abounds with the recognition of the sinfulness of humankind: "All of us like sheep have gone astray, each of us has turned to his own way; but the LORD has caused the iniquity of us all to fall on Him" (Isa. 53:6). "Indeed, there is not a righteous man on earth who continually does good and who never sins" (Eccles. 7:20). "All have sinned and fall short of the glory of God" (Rom. 3:23). "His laws serve only to make us see that we are sinners" (Rom. 3:20 TLB). "If we say that we have no sin, we are only fooling ourselves, and refusing to accept the truth" (1 John 1:8 TLB).

The Focal Point: Jesus Christ

People in the New Testament did not respond to a series of theological propositions. They responded to a person—Jesus Christ. "We have found the Messiah," said Andrew (John 1:41 NEB). "Come, see a man. . . . This is not the Christ, is it?" asked the woman at the well (John 4:29). "We have met the man spoken of by Moses in the law," Philip told Nathaniel (John 1:45 NEB).

The Target for Witness: Responsive People

Jesus told his followers, "As you enter his house, give it your blessing . . . if no one will welcome you or even listen to what you have to say, leave that house or town, and once outside it shake off the dust of that place from your feet" (Matt. 10:12–14 PHILLIPS). Jesus was instructing his disciples to identify receptive people and communicate the Good News to them.

Throughout the New Testament we are instructed to focus on people who are willing to listen and respond: "He who has ears, let him hear" (Matt. 13:19). "Lift up your eyes, and look on the fields, that they are white for harvest" (John 4:35). "The seed sown on good soil is the man who both hears and understands" (Matt. 13:23 PHILLIPS).

In the book *Growth: A New Vision for the Sunday School* the authors note, "Paul's strategy for growth was to find and win responsive people . . . people whom God had prepared."[11] Sharing the Good News with responsive people is a common denominator of New Testament strategy.

The Starting Place: The Person's Need

The message was relevant because it spoke to the person's need. Jesus' ministry of healing focused on people's needs . . . then their healing . . . then their following of Christ. "They that [are] whole need not a physician, but they that are sick" (Matt. 9:12 KJV). The Christian commitment that one sees in Scripture is based not on a series of theological propositions to believe in but on a faith that makes people whole. "He said to her, 'Daughter, your faith has made you well'" (Mark 5:34).

The Instrument of God: People

In most cases God uses people to bring other people to himself. Conversions do not take place in a vacuum. Philip was there to interpret the Scripture for the Ethiopian. Peter was there to help Cornelius. Paul was there to help Lydia. When people in the New Testament came to faith, they came through the influence and help of others.

The Proclamation: The *Kerygma*

There were important elements that composed the first Good News proclaimed by the early church. The *kerygma* (a Greek noun meaning "proclamation" or "preached message") was the earliest gospel Christ's apostles took out to their world. Archibald Hunter reviews the essentials of this kerygma: "The prophesies are fulfilled . . . the Messiah has come. He is Jesus of Nazareth, the servant of the Lord . . . who was crucified according to God's purpose, was raised from the dead on the third day, is now exalted to God's right hand, and will come in glory for judgment. Therefore, repent, believe this Good News, and be baptized for the forgiveness of your sins and the gift of the Holy Spirit."[12]

This message was preached by all the apostles. At Pentecost Peter preached, "Therefore let all the house of Israel know for certain that God has made Him both Lord and Christ" (Acts 2:36–38, 41). Paul proclaimed that through Christ "God was manifest in the flesh, justified in the Spirit, seen of angels, preached unto the Gentiles, believed on in the world, received up into glory" (1 Tim. 3:16 KJV). In 1 Corinthians Paul outlines a summary of the kerygma and then comments, "Whether, then, it was I or they [Peter, James, John, and the rest], this is what we preach" (1 Cor. 15:11 NIV). The basic elements of the message—the kerygma—were proclaimed with the goal of persuading the hearers to repentance, faith, and baptism.

The Motivation: Love

Christ's entire life and ministry was a personification of God's unconditional love. The apostles and early church continued to emphasize this all-encompassing love. The rapid spread of the gospel must have been due in large part to their desire to see others share in such extraordinary love.

The Method: Dialogue and Interaction

The Ethiopian posed questions to Philip about the Scripture passages he was reading (Acts 8:27–29). Paul asked Jesus for a confirmation of his identity (Acts 9:1–9). The Philippian jailer asked, "What must I do to be saved?" (Acts 16:25–35). Cornelius asked the angel and then Peter for an explanation of his vision (Acts 10). The woman at the well asked Christ his identity (John 4:5–30). Nicodemus (John 3:1–21), Zacchaeus (Luke 19:2–10) . . . all interacted and had the opportunity to question, discuss, and consider the claims of Christ.

The Goal: Repentance and Conversion

John the Baptist called for repentance (Matt. 3:2). Jesus' teaching and preaching demanded repentance (Mark 1:15; Luke 13:3). Peter's instructions required repentance (Acts 2:38; 8:22). Paul's message insisted on repentance (Acts 17:30; 26:20). Repentance is an important step, from the biblical viewpoint, in the conversion process. Repentance involves a change of mind and heart, a turning *from.* The other side of repentance is conversion. It is a person's turning *to* God in allegiance, obedience, and faith. In the turning, God regenerates and gives eternal life (2 Cor. 5:17; Rom. 6:23). "Rebirth," "new life in Christ," "obedience to the faith," "hearing the Word of the Gospel," "hearing the Word," "believed," "believed and were baptized"—Scripture uses many terms to describe a person who has moved from death to life, from doubt to faith, from sin to salvation.

The Result: Baptism and Identification with the Church

In the New Testament the rite of incorporation into the body was baptism. Baptism was a crucial part of becoming a Christian. "In fact," observes Steven Smalley, "the New Testament knows nothing of coming into the Body by faith only. It was by faith and baptism. Baptism was the accompanying act of obedience and confession, and without baptism, a believer did not enter the early community of faith."[13]

Sharing Your Faith: Six Suggestions

Here are some suggestions to help you in verbally sharing your faith with others, especially those in your Extended Family. They are built on the biblical examples and models of the verbal part of being a witness.

1. Be Sensitive

Be sensitive to the spiritual needs and receptivity of those in your Extended Family. Skills of listening, of empathy, of identification, of relating the gospel and the church to relevant needs will be of great value in knowing when and how to share the Good News. Asking questions will help you determine where your friends are in their spiritual journey.

2. Be Open to the Holy Spirit's Direction

In most cases God uses people to bring other people to faith. Isn't it exciting that he has chosen you to be a witness of his eternal grace? Isn't it affirming that he believes in you enough to open doors where you can communicate the faith? Closing yourself off to his leadership is unproductive. Opening yourself by saying, "Here I am, Lord; send me" leads to enlarged ministry, usefulness, blessing, and joy.

3. Be Able to Explain the Hope within You

You should be able to testify clearly to your faith (1 Peter 3:15). Describe the events that brought you to repentance, to faith, and into the church. Be confident in expressing why and how Jesus is Lord in your life. Some people find help in writing out their testimony and memorizing it. Others rehearse it with a friend. Whatever means you use, be able to share your experience clearly, concisely, and in words understandable to a non-Christian. "True, it's important to know what and who you believe," says Becky Tirabassi. "But I have found that a personal experience is far more interesting to hear and difficult to refute."[14]

4. Know the Gospel of the Kingdom

Be on speaking terms with the basics of your faith: humanity's sin; Christ's incarnation, death, and resurrection; repentance; faith; and so on. The more appropriate Scriptures you know, the more comfortable you will feel. While proclaiming the gospel is more than simply reciting Bible verses, having a grasp of Scriptures concerning God's love and how one enters into his kingdom is an important part of the process.

5. Use Your Gifts and Those of Others

Identify your spiritual gifts, then supplement yours by using other gifts in the body. The apostle Paul understood this great truth when he said, "I planted, Apollos watered, but God was causing the growth. . . . Now he who plants and he who waters are one; but each will receive his own reward according to his own labor" (1 Cor. 3:6, 8). The Bible is clear that God gives gifts to his church—to his people—and that their purpose is to build up the body (Eph. 4:12). Each member of the body is given different gifts. We do not all have the gift of evangelism—that special ability to share the gospel with unbelievers in such a way that men and

What Is the Gospel?

To five basic questions, the gospel message gives penetrating answers.

1. Who Am I?

Every person, at some point in his or her life, has asked the question, Who am I? What is my identity? God has anticipated this question, and at the very outset of the Bible, in its earliest pages, he addresses it. Indeed, when we open the Bible, we are face-to-face with the great truth of creation. "And God created man in His own image" (Gen. 1:27). Here is God's answer: We have been made in the image and likeness of God himself. We can find our identity in this reality—that we have been created for a relationship with God.

2. How Can I Be Made Fit for God's Presence?

Being made acceptable to him has to do with what Jesus Christ did when he took our guilt and shame and made it his own. He received the judgment we deserved. The Bible calls this the redemptive, atoning work of Christ, and it leads to "justification by faith." By this we mean God accepts us "in his Son," cleansed by the blood of his sacrifice and clothed with the righteousness of Christ. We are thereby declared righteous and are fit for God's presence and fellowship. All this is God's response to humanity's quest for acceptance.

3. Can My Life Be Changed?

The gospel touches on another basic question: Is there any possibility of my character being transformed? Must I always be pushed around by habits I can't control? The good news of the gospel is that through what the Scriptures call "sanctification," through the in-working of God's Holy Spirit, we can put off our old selves. We can put on the new. We do not need to remain the people we once were. Jesus Christ liberates. Jesus Christ sets people free. We can be conformed to the image of Jesus Christ. That indeed is good news!

4. To Whom Do I Belong?

The Good News says, "You belong to a community, the community of God's people, the body of Christ." If we have received Jesus Christ and experienced the new birth, we have the privilege—indeed, the obligation—of relating to all those who have similarly reached out for Jesus Christ. We belong to them and they belong to us. We share a common life. Prior to coming to Christ, we are alone, as solitary individuals. But after coming to Christ, we find we are members of a family, the family of God. And as we participate in the life of a local congregation, we become enriched and strengthened in our Christian life.

5. Is There Hope for the World?

Shall the world always know poverty, war, oppression, and injustice? Christians are to be the salt of the earth. They are to stand against the rottenness of the times. They are to be Christ's presence in the midst of people. They are to work for social justice and for the improvement of the human condition. But more, Christians are to look for the second coming of Jesus Christ. This is the great hope of the church. There is coming a day unlike all other days. And before that day ends, the nations shall know the presence of the Lord and the knowledge of the glory of the Lord "as the waters cover the sea." Then righteousness shall reign. Then sin shall be forever gone. Then all shall witness the new heaven and the new earth.

> So the good news of the gospel provides identity, acceptance, transformation of character by the Holy Spirit; it provides community, belonging, and hope for the world! What good news we have to bring! The gospel is the one message that can satisfy the yearning of human hearts and meet the needs of our world.

women become Jesus' disciples and responsible members of the body of Christians. If you have the gift of evangelism, by all means use it. But if you have the gift of hospitality, prayer, witnessing, teaching, pastoring, wisdom, giving, mercy, helping, or something else, these also can be used for making disciples. Use not only your gifts but those of the body to support you in your witness.

6. Realize the Goal Is Incorporation

Evangelism is not complete until the person is incorporated into the body. The goal of effective evangelism is that the new Christian becomes a disciple and a responsible member of the church. Your disciple-making plan should include the incorporation of your Extended Family members into the body. Incorporation goes beyond formal membership. Effective incorporation, as you will see later in this book, has a variety of dimensions, but the result is that people are active parts of God's family, using their gifts joyously in his service.

Providing a Variety of Exposures

As we just noted, each church member should be able to express comfortably to a non-Christian friend the meaning of Christ in his or her life. A dialogue between two friends on the subject of the church and Christianity would include sharing one's personal experience on the subject. There is an important credibility in such sharing between two respected friends.

At the same time, as you plan ways to communicate God's love to the members of your Extended Family, realize that there are additional ways to communicate the message, ways that are perhaps more persuasive. The pastor, a special evangelistic film, a guest teacher or speaker, or a church member with the gift of evangelism may be able to present the gospel in a more compelling way than you can. Actually, most people who end up as active Christians and responsible church members have heard the gospel more than once, from more than one source, prior to making their decision for Christ. One particular study found that those who were vital Christians and active church members had heard the gospel presented an average of 5.8 times before they made their Christian commitment. This fairly high number was in sharp contrast to the number of times the gospel was heard among people who made a decision but soon became inactive. On the average, church dropouts heard the gospel only twice prior to their decision.

This leads to some important implications about communicating the Good News to your Extended Family members. People who eventually come to Christ and become active members of your church need to have enough exposures to the gospel (and the implications of their life-changing decision) to feel they are making a reasonable decision—one they can live with in the months and years ahead.

To illustrate this important disciple-making principle, suppose you were thinking about purchasing a house. You probably wouldn't buy the house after only one or two brief presentations. You would study the market, have the house appraised, look at the neighborhood, schools, taxes. You would talk with other people, probably "sleep on it" for a while, look at alternatives, and finally, after you felt you understood the implications of your contemplated action, you would make the decision to purchase. So it is—or should be—with the life-changing decision confronting your non-Christian friend. Church growth research shows that the person who makes a Christian decision on the spur of the moment (perhaps at the conclusion of an emotional public meeting or a high-pressure, manipulative presentation) is not likely to continue as an active disciple. There is more hope for the person who has had a number of exposures to various elements of the gospel, has seen Christianity demonstrated in the lives of others, and has considered the important implications of his or her decision.[15]

How do you provide this important variety of Christian and gospel exposures for your Extended Family member? Again, the unique and irreplaceable resources of the local church come into play.

As mentioned previously, bringing non-Christian friends to church-sponsored events serves to both enlarge their view of Christ in people's lives and to help them build friendships with other Christians. But bringing your Extended Family member to church-related events also allows the person to hear and see other aspects of the gospel. A full-blown evangelistic message and invitation is not required (or perhaps even desired) at every church-sponsored event. A brief devotional or prayer at the beginning or end of the event serves the important function of providing the non-Christian with a growing understanding and perspective of the gospel.

This need for a variety of evangelistic exposures means a church needs to provide adequate opportunities for members to bring their non-Christian friends and relatives. Worship services and Sunday school classes may be one means in this process. But other events and material may need to be designed to provide such support to the church member. Films, printed material, special outings and social events, home Bible studies, inquirer's classes, and special interest seminars can be used as ways to provide exposure to the Good News. The key insight is that it is not what the particular means of communication is but rather the number and variety of exposures—how many times and from how many sources has your Extended Family member been exposed to a portion of the Good News through the church? The more exposures the person has, the better the chances are that the person will understand the love of Christ and become a responsible church member. Look for ways to help bring this about.

Having Patience

Exercising patience and consistency is vital in the disciple-making process. Remember that each person in your Extended Family is at a different level of development. Not all fruit ripens at the same time. Arthur Glasser observes, "Human hearts are not all the same. Some are very open; some are quite resistant because they are cluttered up with all sorts of things, so that they have no room for the Lord."[16]

As you are involved in the process of making disciples, it is important to let the Holy Spirit do the work, and not take it upon yourself to force a decision. Paul Little has rightly observed, "No one of us can play God for another person. We can't determine the stage of the Holy Spirit's work in his/her life. It may take several years for him/her to come to the Savior and a long period of disinterest may precede his/her decision. For Christ's sake, we must love them nonetheless. It is the Holy Spirit, not we, who converts an individual."[17]

Trying to manipulate a non-Christian into a decision through a series of dramatic appeals or preconceived steps results in a staggering number of dropouts in a short period of time. Several years ago the nationwide "I Found It" campaign by Campus Crusade resulted in thousands of decisions following a presentation of the "Four Spiritual Laws." Research studies conducted a year later, however, indicated that only three out of every one hundred people who made decisions could be found in a local church.[18]

The "new life" of the unfortunate people who are victims of a quick-sell decision rarely becomes a reality. Such "instant evangelism," as Samuel Southard puts it, "produces many still-born babies."[19]

Helping people understand the implications of God's unconditional love, in their time frame and life situation, requires patience and consistency. It is a process that should not be hurried. View the act of expressing God's love to members of your Extended Family as a continuing part of your everyday life, a process in which you willingly enter into a long-term commitment of your time and energy for seeing your friend come to Christ and the church.

Keith Miller, looking at his own life in terms of communicating God's love to non-Christians, comments, "As I began to read the New Testament accounts, I saw that Christ almost never went out of His way to help anyone. He seems to have walked along and helped the people in His path. He was totally focused on doing God's will and going where God led Him. But He never failed to help the people He met along the way while going where God directed Him. This made for an amazing steadiness and spiritual economy in His direction and ministry. This one change in my perspective made witnessing not a program but a part of a way of life."[20]

Chuck and his neighbor Pete had been enjoying a growing friendship. Before Chuck identified Pete as a member of his Extended Family, the two had had only a casual "hello, how are you?" acquaintance. Chuck knew that Pete's wife was expecting her first baby in a few months and that Pete's favorite recreation was fishing. Beyond that they had seldom talked about anything more than the weather.

But as a result of his commitment to making disciples, Chuck had made it a point to strengthen his friendship with Pete. He had gone fishing with him and had even helped Pete paint his house. Twice he had invited Pete to go on fishing trips with men from the church who shared Pete's fishing passion.

On the day he became a new father, Pete dashed over to tell the news to Chuck and Diane. Later, when the two were alone, Pete spoke confidentially. "You know, Chuck, after my son was born last night, I never felt happier. But it was the craziest thing. I found myself bawling like a baby. Wasn't that stupid?"

"I don't think it was stupid at all," Chuck replied. "I remember I did the same thing when Karen was born."

"No kidding?" Pete asked.

"That's right."

"You know, being a father is kind of new to me," Pete said. "And I've been doing a lot of thinking. I really need to clean up my act. You know, having a kid, that's a heavy responsibility."

Actually, this turn of events caught Chuck without much to say. As he thought about it later, he sort of blew it. Pete was receptive and would have listened had Chuck shared how his faith helped him as a father. But all Chuck said was, "Hey, our church has a really good class for new parents. It deals with a lot of things that are very helpful to new parents. You and Marlene might really get something out of it. Plus, you'd meet couples who are going through the same thing for the first time."

But Chuck's missed opportunity didn't prove to be all that serious, because Pete and his wife joined the class for new parents, which was their first contact with the church.

Later Pete and his wife began attending other church-related activities, including the contemporary worship service. In time both of them made commitments to become disciples of Jesus Christ. As Chuck looked back, he saw that almost one year had elapsed from the time he first identified Pete as a member of his Extended Family until the date of Pete's Christian commitment.

The way in which Pete came to faith and subsequent incorporation into the church is an excellent example of The Master's Plan in action. As the apostle noted, before the harvest there is planting and watering that must be done. And then, in the right season, God gives the increase (see 1 Cor. 3:6–8).

Clarifying Your Convictions

Inherent in the disciple-making activity is the assumption that both you and your church hold important basic convictions. Here are four questions each potential disciple maker should consider, then answer. Clear, strong convictions will increase one's effectiveness in the process of making disciples.

1. What Do You Really Believe?

What are your basic convictions as a Christian? Can you express in plain, simple English what you believe about God? Christ's love? Sin? Salvation?

2. Why Did You Become a Christian?

What was the reason why you made your commitment to become a Christian? Is being a Christian something you would wish for your best friend or worst enemy?

3. Why Are You a Member of Your Church?

Are there benefits to being active in your church? What are they? Is membership in your church something you regularly celebrate? Or do you usually feel it is a burden?

4. Do You Understand Your Commission?

Is the idea of a personal Great Commission something you really believe? Does it apply to you as much as to any other Christian, or is it basically an idea for ministers and missionaries?

If you are not satisfied with your answers, do something about it. If you feel comfortable with your conviction base, you are ready to put faith into practice.

6

Your Church: Partner in Disciple Making

Christ desires that the Good News be proclaimed by his church. Paul writes to the Ephesians, "That the manifold wisdom of God might now be made known through the church . . . in accordance with the eternal purpose which He carried out in Christ Jesus our Lord" (Eph. 3:10–11).

The church is essential to the disciple-making process. The church is not *a* body of Christ but *the* body of Christ, not just *a* bride of Christ but *the* bride of Christ. The church is the central part of God's plan for making his Good News known.

"The church is much like a movie projector that may be in or out of focus," observes Dr. George Peters, in his book *A Theology of Church Growth*. "Its objective is to accomplish the purpose of God. Its concern must be to focus clearly on this purpose and then carefully, wisely pursue that goal. What is God's purpose? It broke through in full radiance and glory in the miracle of incarnation, the sending forth of His only begotten Son to be the Savior of the world and to reconcile that world to God."[1]

In your plans for reaching the members of your Extended Family, your church can play a more significant role than you ever imagined. It can increase immeasurably your effectiveness in communicating the Good News to your friends and relatives and bring a unique resource to helping these people come into active, responsible church membership. Actually, disciple making in The Master's Plan cannot occur without the participation of the local church. The church is as important to effective disciple making as any other element. What do we mean?

Church-Centered Disciple Making

The central role of the church in making disciples is based on an important concept in The Master's Plan. The concept is called "church-centered disciple making."

Church-Centered Disciple Making: An intentional strategy and priority of the church that initiates disciple making, trains members in disciple making, uses resources of the body, creates support resources, and incorporates new believers into the church.

Church-centered disciple making puts the church—as a body—at the center of the evangelism process. It includes the church as a partner in the disciple-making endeavor. Here are seven important contributions the local church makes to effective disciple making.

1. The Church Instills a "Great Commission Conscience"

A "Great Commission conscience" is the conviction among members that their church has the mandate, opportunity, and responsibility to communicate the gospel to those who have yet to believe. In a church with a Great Commission conscience, a disciple-making mentality permeates every facet and organization of its body. The result is that each member has a genuine concern for friends, relations, and neighbors outside Christ. A Great Commission conscience is fostered by church leaders who exhibit enthusiasm for and devotion to making disciples and constantly hold the disciple-making goal up as a priority of the church.

A Great Commission conscience is developed through preaching and Bible study focused on God's unswerving purpose to reach lost people. It is created as members are clearly taught the biblical foundations of caring for and reaching people outside Christ. It is taught in Sunday school classes, in small group fellowship meetings, in women's circles, in home cell groups. It is reflected and modeled in the lives of church officers, boards, committees, men's groups, women's groups, and youth groups. It is a philosophy of ministry that permeates the life of the church. A Great Commission conscience means that the entire church—and all its parts—thinks and acts in response to the Great Commission.[2]

2. The Church Equips Members to Follow the Great Commission

Church leaders have a scriptural mandate to equip the saints for the work of ministry so "God's people will be equipped to do better work for Him, building up the church, the body of Christ, to a position of strength and maturity; until finally we all believe alike about our salvation and about our Savior, God's Son, and all become full-grown in the Lord—yes, to the point of being filled full with Christ" (Eph. 4:12–13 TLB).

The education ministry of your church is a natural place to help members understand the meaning of their faith, how to witness, the basic convictions of the gospel, and how to point a friend to Christ. Peter's words are crystal clear: "Always be ready to give a defense to everyone who asks you a reason for the hope that is in you" (1 Peter 3:15 NKJV).

Helping each member identify and use his or her spiritual gifts is another task of the church in equipping members to fulfill the Great Commission. Not every member has the gift of evangelism, yet each Christian does possess spiritual gifts that can be used in the disciple-making endeavor. The church with a Great Commission conscience uses all the gifts of its members to communicate God's love to others. Spiritual gifts are a means to an end, not an end in themselves. The gifts of the body are to be used in harmony with God's unswerving purpose for his church and his people: the redemption of lost humanity.

Donald McGavran once said, "You would misuse Christ's gifts if you used them solely for service of existing Christians. That is not why these gifts are given. As we see God's overwhelming concern for the salvation of people, we must assume that His gifts are given, at least in large part, that the lost may come to know Him."[3]

3. The Church Helps Members Reach Their Extended Family

The most natural place to begin disciple making in your church is within each member's web of influence. Members of Sunday school classes, home Bible groups, sports teams, deacons, and ushers can all begin to focus on the people in their web and develop plans for seeing them come to Christ and the church.

The local church body has the unique opportunity to help members see that making disciples is the concern of each Christian and that God has given each person a unique opportunity to share his love with certain people.

4. *The Church Provides Motivation, Encouragement, and Accountability*

Members are most effective in disciple making when the church structures regular encouragement, guidance, and accountability into the process. An important part of this support is providing opportunities for regular meetings in which members report progress, share triumphs, and relate experiences. Such church-sponsored "Support Team" groups encourage members in their commitment. As each member of the Support Team shares his or her disciple-making goals and concerns, members feel an important sense of community in their task.

Support Team: A group of church members who are involved in making disciples and meet together regularly to encourage one another and learn how to more effectively communicate God's love to their Extended Family members.

The church can also provide encouragement as it publicly and personally affirms members in their disciple-making efforts. Regular support and visibility of members' disciple-making successes shows that it is significant in the eyes of church leadership and basic to the goals of the congregation.

5. *The Church Complements Disciple-Making Efforts*

As we saw earlier, when non-Christians have a variety of opportunities to hear the gospel and see it demonstrated, there is a greater likelihood that they will eventually become disciples. The church is a unique resource in which

Extended Family members can see the Christian faith demonstrated in a variety of settings, by a variety of people. Programs and activities of the church, such as music performances, recreation and sporting events, special interest groups, mission presentations, and church school learning experiences can creatively exemplify God's love and provide those varieties of exposures. Interaction between Extended Family members and church members is an important part of a successful disciple-making plan.

In his dissertation Dr. Flavil Yeakley analyzed the differences between the decision process of people who continued as active Christian disciples and that of those who soon dropped out. He concluded that "when a person has no meaningful contact with the congregation in the process of his/her conversion, that person is likely to feel no meaningful sense of identification with the congregation after his/her conversion and therefore more likely to drop out."[4] Every opportunity for non-Christians to rub shoulders with church members provides an additional personification of Christ's love. Outsiders catch the warm, caring spirit. They sense the reality of Christ's presence that affects lives.

6. The Church Meets Extended Family Members' Needs

A church effectively supporting members' disciple-making activities will design programming and services around the needs and interests of Extended Family members. Focusing on such areas as single parents, seniors, young married couples, and single young adults can present opportunities for relevant programs and activities in which God's love can be experienced in caring and appropriate ways.

How does a church discover the needs and concerns of Extended Family members so as to plan appropriately? The simplest way is often to ask members involved in the disciple-making process. As church members identify and strengthen their relationships with the members of their Extended Family, they naturally become aware of these people's interests, concerns, life situations, and stressful moments. Lyle Schaller comments, "If you want to find out people's needs, ask them."[5] Communication lines must be kept open between church leaders able to influence programming and members looking to respond to the needs of their Extended Family members.

The time-honored slogan "Find a need and fill it" has direct application for the church concerned with helping members make disciples. In finding needs of Extended Family members, the church discovers opportunities to meet those needs and share God's love as expressed through Jesus Christ.

7. The Church Administers the Disciple-Making Process

"Where there is no vision, the people perish" (Prov. 29:18 AMP). Churches eager to help members discover their hidden disciple-making potential have little problem with morale and involvement as the process begins to flourish. But for those dreams to become a reality, there are important administrative responsibilities to be carried out.

Personnel are necessary to coordinate disciple-making strategy and help implement each step. Making disciples may require "clearing the decks" of competing interests until the process becomes established among groups and individual members in the church.

The commitment to making disciples will be reflected in the church budget. Adequate financial support of programs for disciple making will determine whether the church is sincere in supporting its members. Money on the line means the matter is serious.

Evaluation is an important part of administering the disciple-making process. Church leaders should regularly examine whether the church's disciple-making efforts are bringing fruit, by looking closely at their own experience, other members' experience, and actual results. Through regular evaluation, refinements in strategy can be made to build on the strengths and eliminate the problems. Evaluation should focus on the training process, member involvement, church support, and incorporation effectiveness.

Your Church's "Potential Congregation"

Here is a powerful concept that will help translate church-centered disciple making into a natural part of your church's planning and activities. It is a concept that should soon become a way of thinking for every church leader, officer, and staff member. The concept: your "Potential Congregation."

Potential Congregation: The cumulative group of your church members' Extended Families.

Let's take a closer look at the idea of your church's Potential Congregation, since it has important implications for the success of every church member's plan for reaching his or her Extended Family.

Disciple Making through Your Potential Congregation

The records in your church identify a group of individuals and families who compose the "members of your congregation." These people are listed in the church directory and are people about whom various information is kept. Perhaps their participation in church events is recorded. Most of the activities, programs, and classes planned by church leaders are done so with this group of members in mind. Most church leaders rightly feel that a major function of the church is to care for these members, to be responsive to their needs, and to provide an opportunity for personal and spiritual growth. That is good and is the way it should be. Building up the body is a significant function of the church.

Now consider the implications for your church's ministry if the definition of the "members of your congregation" were expanded. While the responsibilities for service to members would be the same, the membership of the congregation would now include new people—all those people, in fact, in the Extended Families of your present members. It is this group of people that forms your church's Potential Congregation. They are quite winnable and waiting to be won.

In so redefining its congregation, your church enlarges considerably its view of ministry. Your church's concern now extends beyond its present members to include all these potential disciples. Now you are not only serving existing members—who might be called your "Worshiping Congregation"—but as a church, you are responding to and ministering to those who make up your Potential Congregation as well. And like the members of your Worshiping Congregation, the members of your Potential Congregation can be identified by name, information can be gathered on each, needs can be identified, and programs can be developed.

When You Identify Your Potential Congregation

What is the impact of such a view of your church and congregational responsibilities? How will this new view of disciple making affect your church's outreach strategy and planning?

Here are six important implications.

1. Your Church Focuses on Reachable People

The members of your Potential Congregation are people outside the body of Christ but inside the Extended Families of present members; therefore they are closely related to your church. The people within your church's Potential Congregation are more reachable than those not in the webs of present members.

A follow-up study to a Billy Graham Crusade showed the importance of focusing on reachable people. The study, conducted one year following a large crusade, looked for the people who had made a decision during the course of the event, to find out how many were then involved in a local church. It turned out that only fifteen out of every one hundred people who came forward to make a Christian commitment could later be found participating in a local church. However, of those people who were active, *82 percent* had a friend or relative in that church prior to their decision![6] Most of the new converts found in churches one year later had been in the Extended Family of a church member, and part of that church's Potential Congregation. The prior relationship with the church member was the bridge for the new Christian to come into the church and kept that new believer incorporated.

An additional study underscores the fact that friends and relatives are a key in the process of making a religious decision. The Mormon sect keeps accurate records of the successes and failures of its mission endeavors. A study published in the *American Journal of Sociology* reports that the success rate of the Mormon missionaries, who go from door to door calling, is approximately .1 percent (one conversion per one thousand contacts). However, when these same missionaries present the Mormon message in the home of one of their church members to a non-Mormon neighbor, the success rate jumps to 50 percent![7] The article "How to Share the Message with Your Neighbors," published in their national magazine, exemplifies their strategy of encouraging relationships between members and neighbors to convert new people to their beliefs.[8]

2. Your Church Focuses Its Caring Ministry

Caring is a beautiful and important function of the body of Christ. Too often, however, people have to be on the inside to experience it. In your Potential Congregation an exciting new possibility opens to your church. Caring continues to be a major function in the life of the Worshiping Congregation and is still focused on the needs and concerns of its members. However, this caring is now also extended to the members of your Potential Congregation and identifies an important new group of people as recipients of the church's concern. The need to be cared for and loved is common to all individuals. The church that focuses its caring ministry on both present members and potential members will see significant results as those in the Potential Congregation respond to this caring and become new disciples. The church is exemplifying the love of God in his name.

3. Your Church Focuses Its Programming

Most ministries in a church are planned for the members of that congregation. The youth ministry is for the youth in the church. The music ministry is generally for the benefit and involvement of members in the church. The minister of education is paid to organize Christian education to nurture church members.

Recognizing your Potential Congregation will help your church evaluate and prioritize its programming efforts. While programming and ministry are still focused on the needs and interests of members, the expanded definition of "members" now means that programming and planning considerations include Potential Congregation members as well. Of course, not every event in the church is expected to focus on both groups. But over the church year there should be equal consideration given to each group in the overall planning, development, and appropriation of church resources.

In the planning of programs, special events, and seminars, the unique needs and interests of members in your church's Potential Congregation should be carefully considered. Because the needs and interests of non-Christians differ, don't assume that all members of your Potential Congregation will respond to one type of programming. Just as not every member of your Worshiping Congregation would be interested in the women's brunch or the young marrieds' class or the singles' retreat, potential disciples will have a variety of interests as well. In planning ministry to your Potential Congregation, take into account the unique qualities of these potential disciples. They have special concerns and interests, family situations, certain images of the church and its people. It is around the unique needs of both Worshiping Congregation members and Potential Congregation members that your church should concern itself in planning for effective ministry.

4. Your Church Experiences Increased Morale

A minister of evangelism recently related to us the tremendous change in morale that resulted from his church's successful strategy to reach out to friends and relatives. "At first, when the new members were presented to the congregation for baptism," he recalled, "most people in the church didn't quite know what to do. It had been a long time since that many people had joined the church at one time. But as the months went on and more friends and relatives began coming to Christ and the church, it really started to sink in. Older members began to believe that maybe the church did have something to offer outsiders. As they heard the new Christians testify to the joy and excitement of their new faith, it really turned a lot of attitudes around. It's been like a snowball picking up momentum as it rolls down the hill—it just keeps building on itself!"

Contagious enthusiasm and excitement invariably result when members see their longtime friends and relatives come into new life in Christ and their church. Morale also builds as the new Christians, who are invariably enthusiastic about their newfound faith, become active in the church. Making disciples and reaching the members of your Potential Congregation can uncover new dimensions of spiritual growth and vitality that you may never have thought existed in your church.

5. Your Church Invests Resources Effectively

A concern of church leaders is good stewardship of resources. Poor stewardship invests the church's time, money, and most valuable commodity—people—in areas that do not produce a return. Yet as we saw at the beginning of this book, much time and many people are being invested in methods of evangelism that do not result in a good harvest. This does not happen when resources are invested and focused on a church's Potential Congregation. These potential disciples have been identified as one of the most receptive groups of people in your community. It is simply good stewardship to respond to the people God has prepared and do our part in bringing them into the kingdom.

Because your church has identified these groups of people (members' Extended Families) to whom you seek to communicate God's love, you can accurately evaluate the effectiveness of various ministries in terms of new Christian disciples. Some approaches and programs for these people will be more effective than others. Effective strategy should be based on the ministries that bring results.

6. Your Church Continually Expands

As members of your Potential Congregation make a commitment to Christ and become members of the body and the Worshiping Congregation, they each have their own web of influence. As these new disciples are helped in their disciple-making plans, they identify members in their Extended Families and as a result increase the size of the Potential Congregation. So the process begins all over again. This is exactly the way the early church grew—first by addition (Acts 2:47), then by multiplication (Acts 6:7).

The various Support Team members had been taking turns hosting the biweekly meetings. Chuck and Diane arrived at Bob Odman's apartment and spent a few minutes in informal fellowship before Tim, the team coordinator, convened the meeting.

One by one the various members shared what had been happening in their disciple-making endeavors since their previous meeting. Steve told about his cousin, whom he was focusing on, and how they had gone out for a hamburger one evening last week. "We didn't talk about religion or anything," Steve said, "but we're starting to get to know each other a lot better. We've shared some personal feelings, and there's a good level of trust building."

"Sounds encouraging," Tim said. "Have you introduced your cousin to anyone else in the church?"

"No. I guess I should do that," Steve said. "Let's see now . . ."

"How about the softball team?" asked Diane. "Does he like softball?"

"No, he's more of an intellectual type. He wouldn't go for those simple, mundane things." Steve looked over at Bill, the pitcher on the softball team.

"Hey!" retorted Bill. "Softball is a very intellectual activity. Not everyone can play, you know."

"Does he like chess?" asked Sue.

"Yeah, he loves it. But do any of you guys play chess?"

"No," said Chuck. "But you know, maybe the church ought to have a chess league. It might be a neat thing to invite our Extended Family members who like chess."

"That would be a great way to introduce them to other people in the church, too," added Steve.

"Good idea. I'll make a note of that and talk to Dave Johnson about it," said Tim, referring to the associate pastor of the church.

After the discussion about Steve's cousin, another member of the group spoke up. "As you know, I've been working with two people in my web—my sister Helen and my next-door neighbor Jim Herman. To tell you the truth, I'm kind of frustrated. It seems like nothing much has been happening in the last couple months, particularly with my neighbor."

"What seems to be the problem?" asked Tim.

"Well, you see, I don't have much in common with him."

"I know what you mean," said Chuck. "When I was focusing on my neighbor Pete, all he ever talked about was fishing. I hate fishing. I almost gave up. But one time I brought Andrew along. He loves fishing. Well, he and Pete hit it off pretty well. Maybe you could introduce your neighbor to someone in the church that might have more in common with him."

"He does have a thing about gardening, especially flowers. Tim, you play in the dirt, don't you?"

"Well, I enjoy gardening, if that's what you mean," said Tim. "You know, there's a horticultural show down at the center next week. Why don't I stop by and see if he wants to go? You ought to go along, too, though."

"Sure, I'll go."

The meeting went on another thirty minutes, with other members sharing the progress of their disciple-making efforts and talking through additional plans for communicating God's love to each Extended Family member. Some of the members reported real progress, while others had to be encouraged to "wait on the Lord."

Tim then led the group in a fifteen-minute Bible study. They had been studying various personalities in the New Testament and how each had responded to the Great Commission. This evening they were studying the apostle Barnabas.

Following the Bible study, Tim passed out copies of a sheet listing upcoming church-sponsored activities that might be appropriate for members to use in their disciple-making plans. The sheet listed various sports events, social outings, and seminars that had all been designed to be part of the church's disciple-making support strategy.

The group concluded with prayer for each Extended Family member mentioned that night, then set the time and place for the next Support Team meeting.

7

Incorporating New Disciples into the Church

This was the night for paying monthly household bills. Those who knew Chuck well, like Diane and his daughter, Karen, made it a point to avoid the den that entire evening. To make matters worse, Chuck's calculator had expired with only half the bills paid.

Then the phone rang. Chuck didn't even try to hide his frustration. The caller was Mary, his sister.

Diane walked by the door just as the phone rang, and looked in to see an amazing sight. Chuck was smiling! And what was more unusual, there were tears in his eyes.

A very curious Diane broke the long-standing family rule and entered Chuck's den to find out what was going on.

Chuck hung up the phone, turned to Diane, and continued to smile.

"Sweetheart, that was Mary. She's just recommitted her life to Christ, and she's going to join the church!"

Diane gave her husband a warm hug. "And to think that just a little over a year ago you were insisting you couldn't possibly be a witness!"

"Well, much as I hate to admit it, I guess I was wrong."

"Did I hear you say you were wrong? Now that is hard to believe."

Another phone call saved Chuck from having to respond. It was Pastor Austin.

"Yes, Pastor, she did call. Yes, I do understand my responsibility for both of them."

What Pastor Austin was reminding Chuck about was the importance of successfully incorporating new disciples like Pete and Mary into the church.

"Unless they become responsible members of the church and assume their place in the body," the pastor said, "the disciple-making process is incomplete."

Incorporation: Some Assumptions

It is true. Evangelism is not complete without the new Christian becoming an active part of the church. There are some important things to remember about the process of incorporating a new member. Consider Mary, for example.

1. Mary's incorporation will not be automatic. Laity often assume that newcomers to the church will naturally look for and find a place in one group or another and be immediately accepted by members of that group. As the old saying goes, "It ain't necessarily so." It is often surprisingly difficult for a newcomer to find a place where he or she fits and feels a sense of belonging. Most groups do not automatically reach out and incorporate the newcomer. As a result there is often a high "mortality rate" among new Christians. The new believer's need for caring and nurturing is analogous to a new baby's requirement for much care and feeding and special attention. Just as the new baby cannot survive without the help of others, the new Christian needs help to begin his or her new life.

2. The church, rather than Mary, is responsible for her incorporation into the body. Most new Christians join a church with the expectation of growing into active and contributing members. They want to learn and grow and build meaningful relationships in their new church home. If they never become active church members, the problem usually can be traced to the church rather than the new member. Monitoring the new Christian's involvement in the church, particularly during the first few critical months, should be a regular practice of the church body and its various organizations. If new Christians drop out of a church, in most cases the church has failed in its responsibility.

3. The people who brought Mary to Christ have the primary responsibility to help her become an active member. Friends or relatives already in a church make all the difference in incorporating that new member into the church. When the new Christian sees familiar faces in this new environment and has friends who help him or her build new relationships with others, assimilation takes place much more naturally.

4. Mary's incorporation began before membership. The incorporation process of a new disciple starts long before the person joins the church. The friendships established with others in the church earlier in the disciple-making process now serve as a natural bridge into the Worshiping Congregation. Extended Family members who earlier became part of a group in the church are incorporated before they formally join the church. According to Lyle Schaller, among those not related to a congregation by kinship, those most likely to remain active have become part of a small group in which membership in that group was important, before formally uniting with that congregation.[1] They are assimilated before they join the church.

5. Mary's incorporation must be a high priority for the church. There is no great accomplishment in fulfilling the Great Commission if people coming in the front door of the church are exiting out the back door. A commitment of time, money, and people is necessary for a church to have an effective incorporation strategy and for Extended Family members to find a place they can call home. Providing for the development and growth of new members and equipping them for ministry are necessary steps in making disciples.

Incorporation: A Church-Centered Strategy

How do we insure that new Christians become integrated into the life of the congregation, that they develop a sense of belonging and identity and become an active part of the church's life and ministry?

The question of incorporation is crucial. A strategy for successful incorporation of new members is a major part of any church's commitment to making disciples. A church-centered approach to incorporation rightly assumes the centrality of the church in this process.

Here are six steps to seeing an effective incorporation strategy become a reality in your church.

1. Build an "Incorporation Consciousness"

A church with an incorporation consciousness is one in which people go out of their way to greet the newcomer and get to know him or her, in which they do everything possible to make the person feel welcome and an important part of the church. In most churches, however, an incorporation consciousness does not naturally occur. And while many a congregation likes to think of itself as a "friendly church," a first-time visitor might have quite a different impression. Often small groups in a church, without realizing it, exclude and even isolate newcomers. A conscious and continuous effort must be made, therefore, to encourage laity and groups in the church to be open to outsiders. Building an incorporation consciousness is not difficult. But it requires a high priority on the part of church leaders, officers, and members. Incorporation of new members should be a regular item on the agenda of most board and officers' meetings. Sunday school class sessions, small group meetings, worship services, and midweek prayer meetings should frequently stress to each layperson the importance of being open and caring to the newcomer.

2. Develop an Incorporation Structure

More and more churches, seeing the need for a formal concern for the incorporation of new members, are establishing an assimilation committee. Here are some suggestions for organizing a system to incorporate new members into your church.

- Establish a "new member tracking committee," composed of laypeople, that is exclusively concerned with overseeing the first nine months of each new member's life in the church. The committee keeps accurate, updated records on every new member. It provides information to each class or small group when patterns of inactivity are discerned.
- Appoint a person in each class and small group in the church to be responsible for the incorporation of new people. Such a person is responsible to see that new people are introduced to others in the group and that the class or group is open to accept them.

Do You Have an Incorporation Problem?

Consider your church and answer the following questions.

1. Are there large numbers of "transfers out" who keep the same residency?
2. Do more than 50 percent of the people in your church have no specific role, task, or small group identification?
3. Is there a large gap between church membership and average worship attendance?
4. Is there a large gap between Sunday school enrollment and Sunday school attendance?
5. Do a high percentage of members attend worship service one Sunday per month or less?
6. If you were to ask them, would many of the members say they feel left out?
7. Are there large numbers of visitors who do not come back?
8. Is there a high percentage of new members who were not exposed to the ministries and people of your church prior to their joining?
9. Are there large numbers of new members who do not have a friend or relative in the church?
10. Are there members whose level of involvement suddenly declines?
11. Do your members have needs that are appropriate for the church to meet but are not being met?

If the answer to many of the questions is yes, you may have an incorporation problem and should consider ways to solve it.

- Research previous incorporation results. Analyze the present level of involvement of people who joined the church in the last two years. How many are now active church members, and how many have dropped out? Studying the patterns of incorporation gives unique insights into present strengths and weaknesses of your church's incorporation methods.
- Interview once active but now inactive members to find out why they dropped out. Lessons learned from these people are valuable in alleviating potential problems for future members.

3. Provide Friendship-Building Opportunities

As we have seen, the number of close friends a new member develops in the church has a direct influence on whether he or she continues as an active member. If after six months the new member can identify few or no close friends in the church, the chances are high that the person will soon be inactive. But if the new member has a growing number of close friends who are active in the church, it will be unusual for that person to drop out. The "friendship factor," research tells us, is the most important element in determining whether a person remains active in a local church or drops out.

What does this mean for your church? One implication is that church groups should provide opportunities for building friendships among members. Organize activities that are just plain fun, activities that strengthen personal ties between members. Be sure that both old members and new members (and potential new members) attend. The event should not be just a social occasion to entertain the same old gang.

An effective incorporation strategy will help new members build additional relationships beyond the friend or relative responsible for bringing the person to Christ. You will know your incorporation strategy is working when you see new members continue as active members even when their friend or relative moves to another city or goes on to be with the Lord.

4. Structure Need-Meeting Ministries

Focus on the unique needs that new members bring to the church: personal, spiritual, marital, occupational, and relational needs. Life is full of problems. Becoming a Christian and member of a church does not mean all problems go away. But the Christian faith does provide a deep pool of strength from which to draw in coping with problems. A church concerned with seeing people grow and mature in the Christian life should have ministries that directly respond to the needs of its members—particularly its new members.

Starting new groups is an excellent way to provide such support. Groups or classes may be topically oriented and deal with areas of concern to members. A list of such need-meeting classes might look like this:

Personal

- How to Reduce Weight
- How to Stop Smoking
- Coping with Stress
- Feeling Good about Yourself
- Self-Discipline: Why and How

Spiritual

- What the Bible Says About . . .
- How to Share Your Faith with Your Friends
- Daily Bible Study: Why and How

- Discovering and Using Your Spiritual Gifts
- Prayer: Is Anyone Listening?

Marital
- Communicating with Your Spouse
- Your Marriage: The First One Hundred Days
- New Parents' Class
- Coping with Divorce and Remarriage
- Children and Drugs

Occupational
- Dealing with Job-Related Anxiety
- Working in a Non-Christian Environment
- Re-entering the Job Market
- Changing Jobs

Relational
- Learning to Listen
- How to Deepen Your Friendships
- Dating and the Christian
- Coping with In-Laws

Obviously, there are many others. And the ministries provided will vary according to members' age, marital status, personal interests, and particular needs. The best way to identify appropriate groups or topics is to form a committee responsible for identifying various areas of need to which the church can respond. If your Great Commission conscience is beginning to develop, you will see that such need-meeting ministries can not only serve new members but also provide ideal opportunities to introduce Extended Family members to the church and its people.

5. Create New Roles and Tasks

How many opportunities for role or task involvement presently exist in your church? In a typical church of 300 members there are approximately eighty such opportunities for laity to fill a role or task. Three-fourths of those present roles are usually filled by 10 percent of the members, who have several jobs each. The remaining roles are filled by members who have only one role or task. So in the typical church of 300 members, 50 members are filling some kind of role or task, leaving 250 members with neither. This is a church structured for nongrowth. Members who have no specific responsibilities can't get involved if they want to; there just aren't enough roles to go around.

There is a direct relationship between the number of roles or tasks available in a church and the number of new people the church can incorporate. According to one study of churches effectively incorporating new people, an ideal ratio of roles or tasks to members is fifty-five per one hundred.[2] That is, for every one hundred adult members there should be at least fifty-five different roles or tasks available. The study also found that in churches with a high dropout rate of new members, the ratio of roles to members was twenty-seven per one hundred, and often lower.

What does this principle of incorporation mean for your church? One implication is that new roles and tasks should be created at the same or greater rate as the number of new members being added. These new roles and tasks should obviously be fulfilling and meaningful to the people involved. The new roles should also have a direct contribution to achieving the goals that the church has established. Providing responsibilities for new members can open to them challenging opportunities of service and ministry through the church—ministry that perpetuates and expands the disciple-making effectiveness of the congregation.

6. Monitor Incorporation Results

A key and ongoing part of effective incorporation involves monitoring new members' involvement in the church. Systematically observing worship attendance, Sunday school attendance, and involvement in small group meetings provides important clues as to the new member's feeling of satisfaction with his or her church life. Closely monitor the involvement levels of each new member for the first nine months of his or her life in the church, and respond immediately at the first sign of problems.

"Sure," you're probably saying, "that's nice in theory, but do you realize what that really means?"

Yes, it's a considerable undertaking. In fact, monitoring incorporation patterns is a job most churches do little or nothing about, simply because of the size of the task. Yet doesn't it seem reasonable that if we are concerned with reaching people and making disciples, we should be equally concerned with seeing that these people are effectively incorporated into the life of the body? Remember the first assumption about the incorporation of Chuck's sister Mary: It is not automatic.

So how do you in a practical way monitor the involvement of the new member?

Keep records of attendance in classes or small group functions. A designated attendance taker can quickly tally members and visitors present and later analyze patterns of participation. Worship service attendance patterns are also important to watch. Studies show that a person's fluctuating attendance at the worship service is the best barometer to indicate that he or she is beginning the dropout process. Here are some suggestions as to how churches can monitor worship service attendance:

- Each Sunday school class and small group in the church can appoint a person to check the worship service attendance of members in their group. The names of church members not involved in any small group are assigned to other people to check.
- Growing numbers of churches (and not just those with over a thousand members) are finding that name tags have a valuable function in the worship service. Not only do name tags make it easier for newcomers to learn and remember names, they provide a creative way to check attendance at the worship service. Each week members pick up their name tags from a rack as they enter the church (they return them on the way out). During the service an usher records the badges still on the rack and keeps a record of members not present (or those not wearing their name tags, which is almost as bad!).
- Many churches place printed cards in the pews or chairs. Members and visitors alike fill them out and drop them in the offering plate or pass them down the aisle.
- A clipboard passed down each aisle is an excellent way to encourage every person to indicate his or her attendance.

What do you do with your list of members who were not in church last Sunday?

If the person is a new member and came into the church through the Extended Family of someone in the church, the best step is to communicate the situation to the original church member. He or she can then look into why the person was not in attendance. There may also be one or more people in the church who are on a friendly basis with the new member. Let them know about the situation, and encourage them to find the reason for the fluctuating involvement level. If there is no one in the church on a friendly basis with the new member (which should give you a good indication of why he or she may be dropping out), encourage someone from a small group in the church, someone with a common interest or age, to call.

A disciple of Jesus Christ is one who is active in the body of Christ, growing spiritually, and then identifying and reaching out to members of his or her Extended Family. The growing cycle of new disciples continues when new members become active and involved in the life of the local church. Incorporating new believers into the fellowship of the Worshiping Congregation should be a priority of the church.

Characteristics of an Incorporated Member

Six months after his sister Mary joined the church, Chuck was optimistic about her growing level of involvement and identification with the church. He had good reason to be, based on the way Mary conformed to the nine characteristics of an incorporated member.

1. Identifies with the Goals of the Church

A clear statement of the goals and priorities that the church holds as central to its purpose will provide an important point for members (especially new members) to rally around. For many newcomers, these goals are the only thing they have in common with other members. The specific goals of a church should

1. be directed toward accomplishing the purpose for which the church exists.
2. be clearly measurable and achievable and include events and activities that will reach those goals.
3. be communicated clearly to church members (especially new members).
4. describe how people can become involved.

The goals should be reviewed yearly. New members should be encouraged to become involved in and identified with one or more of these goals.

One of the first topics of the new members' class that Mary was participating in concerned the stated philosophy and goals of the church. Pastor Austin presented the statement of purpose for the church and how the various programs and ministries all related to this purpose. He then explained the importance of each member's commitment to these directives through various opportunities for involvement.

2. Attends Worship Service Regularly

Nearly everyone would agree that an active, responsible church member participates regularly in a worship service. For most Christians, Sunday morning is the focal point in the church calendar. It is that designated time when the people of God come together to worship him and to strengthen the churchwide celebration of the Christian faith. A new Christian not participating in the worshiping life of the church is certainly missing a critical time of corporate and personal "feeding" and growing in the Word.

In the six months since Mary committed her life to Christ, she had missed only one worship service. She had even taken part in several of the services, reading the Scripture and reporting on the "new neighbor outreach" program she was involved in.

3. Experiences Spiritual Growth and Progress

It is important for every Christian to feel a sense of movement and spiritual growth. This is especially true for the new Christian, who has so much to learn about this new life in Christ. Formal as well as informal Christian education should begin immediately. A special class for new Christians is always valuable in helping them understand their new faith.

Chuck could see almost daily growth in Mary's spiritual life. The Bible study group she was part of on Thursday mornings was a big part of her week. Mary was enthusiastically involved in her Sunday school class, which was studying the Book of Romans, and she was starting to tell Chuck things she had learned in her study that even Chuck didn't know.

4. Becomes a Member of the Body

Different churches have different procedures for officially welcoming a new member into the fellowship. For some it is baptism. For others it is a special service. In still other churches it is a time of personal testimony to the congregation. Whatever that formal step may be, it is important that the new Christian take it soon after his or her Christian commitment and thus officially identify with the body. Such a step gives the new Christian a sense of new beginning. It also gives the church body formal notification that a new member is in their presence and that they should be open and welcoming toward that new member.

Following her recommitment to Christ and instruction by Pastor Austin on what it meant to be a Christian and member of that church, Mary had been presented to the church for membership and baptism. Following the service, she and fourteen other new members were the guests of honor at a church picnic. There Mary and the others each gave their personal testimony of how they had come to Christ. Eleven of the new members reflected on how some person or persons in the church had played an important part in their coming to Christ and the church. It was an exciting and rewarding time for everyone involved.

5. Has New Friends in the Church

The number of new Christian friends a person makes during the first six months of his or her church life directly influences whether that person continues as an active member or drops out. The following table shows one hundred people who recently made a Christian decision—fifty who are now active in their church and fifty who have since dropped out. The table compares the number of friends each group made in the church during the first six months.[3]

Notice the difference between the number of new friends the active members could identify (for example, 13 of the now-active members could identify 7 new friends; 12 active members could identify 8 new friends; 12 could identify 9 or more) and the number of new friends the dropouts could claim. Most active members could identify seven or more new friends in the church; most dropouts only two or less.

The three thousand-member Lake Avenue Congregational Church (Pasadena, Calif.), in seeking to encourage the development of these important relationships, has identified a major function of their Christian education classes and written it in their philosophy of ministry statement:

Number of New Friends	Actives	Dropouts
0	0	8
1	0	13
2	0	14
3	1	8
4	2	4
5	2	2
6	8	1
7	13	0
8	12	0
9+	12	0

"They are to function relationally, as congregations, providing the necessary feeling of belonging and togetherness, providing social functions appropriate for each age level, providing social concern and practical care for the members."[4]

After three months Mary could name five new friends she felt close to and went out with regularly. After six months she could identify nine new friends in the church, and she was beginning to feel quite comfortable in the groups and meetings in which she participated.

6. Has an Appropriate Task or Role

A role is an officially appointed or elected position for a person in the church, such as serving on an ad hoc committee or a board, welcoming visitors, or leading a Bible study. A task is a special, goal-oriented assignment, such as helping with the planning of a church worship service, helping to repave the parking lot, or working on a special missions project.

The more roles available to be filled, the more members can be involved. Once the roles have been created, church leaders' responsibility is to effectively assign roles to people with an appropriate spiritual gift. A variety of resources are available today to help members discover their spiritual gifts. As older members and newer members begin to discover their spiritual gifts, they are invariably drawn to tasks for which God has equipped them.

Mary had accepted the role of host in her Sunday school class. It was her duty to be the first to greet visitors who came to the class. She would learn their names and introduce them to others in the class. Mary had participated in a spiritual gifts discovery course and found she had the gift of hospitality. So she had become part of a "new neighbor" program in which church members invited those who were just moving into the community to their house for dinner. Mary was enjoying her new roles and feeling fulfilled as a contributing member of the church.

7. Is Involved in a Fellowship Group

One of the most meaningful, rewarding, growing experiences the new Christian will have is in a small group within the church, in which the caring, loving fellowship of the body can occur. This small group involvement should be one of the first concerns of the church for its new members.

Organizing and regularly starting groups for new members can be an effective strategy of incorporation. Often a new member will become active in a new group as a "pioneer," whereas it might be difficult for him or her to break into an existing group, in which relationships are already established.

Mary fit easily into the Sunday school class in which two of her friends were already members. She had even met several others in the class before, from previous church events she had attended. Mary also enrolled in the new members' class, and now six other new members and she were meeting for Bible study every Thursday morning.

8. Regularly Tithes to the Church

"Where your treasure is, there will your heart be also" (Matt. 6:21). An important part of any member's responsibility to the church is financial support of its ministries. Regular stewardship should be stressed as a part of commitment to Christ and the church.

Mary is not wealthy, but she has been faithfully tithing each month since she joined the church.

9. Participates in the Great Commission

A disciple of Jesus Christ is one who is involved in spreading the Good News to the members of his or her Extended Family.[5] New Christians are some of the most enthusiastic people in the world. Many have just turned around 180 degrees in their lifestyle and are so excited with their new faith that their enthusiasm results in a natural pattern of friends and relatives coming to Christ and the church over a very short period of time. This natural desire to tell others should be encouraged.

One of the last topics in Mary's new member class was the importance of disciple making as a part of Christ's call. Pastor Austin introduced the fact that each person has a group of close friends and relatives who are potential disciples. Every person in the class was encouraged to identify the people in their Extended Family and develop disciple-making plans for reaching them. Mary had identified Cheryl Riley, a neighbor in her next-door apartment, as a person to focus on. Mary had already begun building a stronger relationship with Cheryl and had told her of the new life she had found.

An effective strategy for incorporating new members should go hand in hand with an outreach strategy to friends and relatives. Through study, evaluation, planning, and regular monitoring of the incorporation process new levels of growth and ministry will be realized in your church, and new Christians can find there a home and a place to grow.

8

The Master's Plan: To the Ends of the Earth

It was already well into Saturday when Chuck finished servicing his car. What had started out as a simple lube and oil change at home to save money had turned into a horrendous task. Chuck was covered with grease from head to toe and was bone weary. But at last he had done it all himself.

He was looking forward to a nice, hot shower, and contemplating sleeping in on Sunday morning. It had been years since the last time he had missed church. But with The Master's Plan working so well, Chuck was anticipating some time off from disciple making. After all, half of his Extended Family members were now disciples with Extended Families of their own.

The warm water felt good on his stiff, aching muscles, and he was giving himself a generous covering of soap lather when Diane called.

"It's Pastor Austin. He has to talk to you immediately. He has to leave in five minutes for an emergency at County Hospital, but he insists he has to talk to you first."

"But I'm all covered with soap."

Well, that's how Chuck ended up standing in a puddle of soapy water by the kitchen phone, clothed in a soggy, soapy robe. He tried to sound cheerful.

"Yes, Pastor, what can I do for you?"

Pastor Austin was calling to make sure Chuck could attend a special committee meeting the following morning. The only time he could arrange that was "convenient" for everyone involved was thirty minutes prior to the early service. "It won't take long, but we've got to get moving in some new areas."

"But I thought now that things were going so well, some of us old-timers at this disciple-making business could start taking things a little easier. After all, my Extended Family is half discipled. Why, we've almost got the Great Commission fulfilled!"

Pastor Austin gave what Chuck thought to be a surprising answer. "Well, we're thankful for what's been done so far, but did you know that we have only just begun?"

"What do you mean?"

"For one thing, all of us old-timers need to get additional members into our Extended Families. And then we need to be sure disciple making becomes the concern of all groups in the church. Then I'm starting to wonder if we don't need to think about sponsoring at least one new church. And of course, there's always our overseas ministry. Well, I've got to get to the hospital. See you in the morning."

The surprising thing was that Chuck didn't act the least bit upset with this unexpected change of plans. There are some that say Chuck Bradley isn't the same since he's been involved in The Master's Plan. Diane says he's discovered that disciple making is one of the most rewarding aspects of the Christian's life.

As long as there are people yet unreached, Christ's command to make disciples remains.

Steps for Expanded Disciple Making

1. Utilize New Christians

If you have met any new Christians recently, you know that their enthusiasm and excitement with their new life in Christ is contagious. They are the happiest people in the world and want the world to know. Life in Christ grants one a refreshing new lease on life. So many older Christians have forgotten what it was like B.C. (before Christ).

As a church leader, how do you broaden your church's disciple-making endeavors? A natural place to begin is among the new converts. New Christians have many new contacts often denied to established members.

Figure 3 illustrates a surprising yet natural phenomenon that occurs in every church. The circle represents the church. The pyramid represents the world. A person at the bottom of the pyramid represents a person who is in the world but outside the church.

When a person becomes a Christian and a church member, he or she still has a good number of contacts and friends in the world. As time passes, however, the now older Christian maintains fewer and fewer contacts in the world and more and more contacts in the church. The reason is simply that as a Christian, he or she feels more comfortable associating with other Christians. New life in Christ is not often compatible with the lifestyle of old friends outside the church.

Many growing churches have discovered the fact that new converts have more contacts with unchurched prospects than do longtime members. As a result, these churches have found ways to effectively train the new

Figure 3

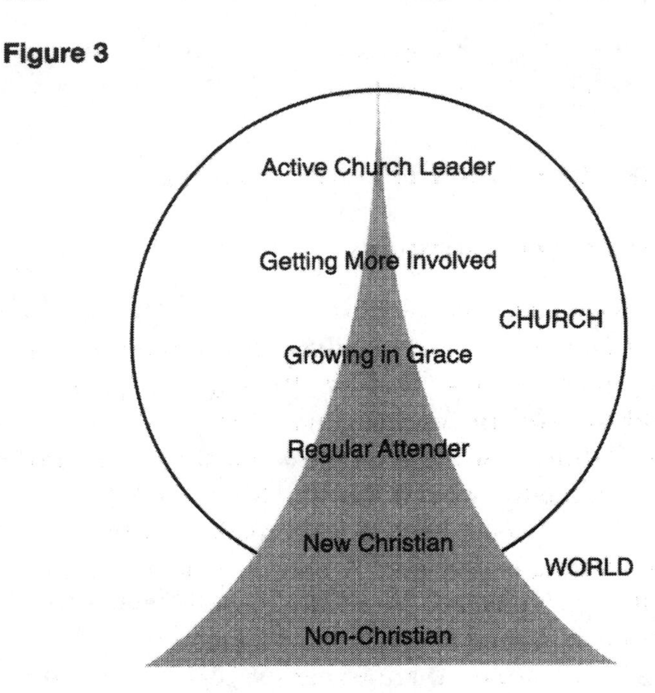

Christians in how to communicate the Good News to their friends.

Helping new Christians focus on their webs is particularly important in reaching members of their immediate family. Why is reaching the new Christian's immediate family so critical?

1. A natural bridge exists to those outside Christ and the church, through the family members already participating.
2. Family members are very responsive and winnable when properly approached.
3. If the family is not reached, the possibility increases tremendously that the one Christian family member will eventually drop out of the church.

Thousands of churches that emphasize a bus ministry to children will testify to the great losses that occur unless the entire family is reached.

4. When the whole family is in Christ and the church, its support system in the home provides encouragement, unity, and Christian growth. The opposite is often true in the non-Christian home.
5. The family itself is strengthened when all members are moving in the same direction rather than creating division and fragmentation.

What attracts families and new people to the faith is the love of Christ, the moving of the Holy Spirit, and the caring fellowship of the local church. When a new Christian can express that power to his or her unreached family members, it is an effective beginning to reaching the entire family.

2. Expand to All Groups in the Church

Effective disciple making does not stop with new Christians trained and involved in reaching out. Disciple making does not stop with only one segment of the congregation trained or involved. The Master's Plan calls for every disciple of Christ to communicate God's love and caring to his or her Extended Family.

As one accumulates experience in building a church-centered strategy of disciple making, additional training sessions should begin. Those members who have been previously involved in The Master's Plan will be excellent references to help other members become God's source for communicating his love. The goal of disciple making in the church should be to see every member involved in communicating God's love and making disciples. This means helping each layperson identify the people in his or her Extended Family and begin praying for them, caring for them, and planning to see them come to Christ and the church.

One way to facilitate the disciple-making process among longtime members is to help them build new relationships. We have stated that longtime Christians usually have few contacts with non-Christians. Does this mean they are absolved of responsibility to reach new people? Of course not! But it does mean that a deliberate attempt may be needed to build new relationships with people outside Christ.

Here is an example of the web-building process in action.

> The United Methodist Church in Carmel, Indiana, developed a strategy of identifying people who moved into its ministry area, and then intentionally built relationships with them and church members. On a large map in the church, the community was divided into areas, sections, and sub-sections. One person or family from the church was assigned to a particular sub-section. (Members were assigned to a sub-section in which they lived.) Each sub-section was several blocks long. The members were then responsible for staying alert to any new people or families who moved into their sub-section. Members were encouraged to immediately introduce themselves to their new neighbors, welcome them, invite them to dinner, develop a friendship, and be alert to ways the church could respond and reach out to these new people. The program has been identified by church leaders as a major factor in the consistent growth of the church.[1]

3. Begin New Groups in the Church

New groups produce new growth. Regularly starting new groups increases your church's effectiveness in disciple making. Here are eight reasons why new groups should be regularly established.

1. New groups provide a positive response to the broad range of human needs.
2. New groups are often more effective in incorporating people into a caring fellowship.
3. New groups enlarge the church's appeal to different kinds of people.
4. New groups are needed to replace those groups that have stagnated or have reached their growth potential.
5. New groups provide Christians with meaningful involvement and service opportunities.
6. New groups discourage clustered, self-serving attitudes and programs.
7. New groups are usually more effective in winning new people to Christ and the church.
8. New groups help the "single cell" church (less than 125 members) begin the process of cell multiplication and growth.

New groups should be designed with appeal to homogeneous groups of people (newlyweds, young singles, senior singles, women re-entering the job market, widows, and so on). As a greater number of diverse groups become part of the church, different kinds of people will be able to find a home in the larger body. Endeavor to match the new groups with the variety of people in your Potential Congregation and Worshiping Congregation. Any kind of person should be able to find a place in your church through becoming incorporated into a small, homogeneous group in which he or she feels comfortable.

4. Start a New Church

The "Great Commission goal" is defined as "a cell [church] of committed Christians in every community, in

Starting New Groups

Here are nine simple steps to starting new groups in your church.

1. Define the target group of people to whom you will minister.
2. Research the target audience and the kind of ministry that would most likely respond to their needs.
3. Find a committed layperson willing to be involved in starting such a group. The person should be similar to the target group.
4. Train this person in the logistics of starting a new group.
5. Begin the member-recruiting process prior to the first group session.
6. Find an appropriate meeting place.
7. Stress the importance of the first several months. They are critical to the success of the group.
8. Keep accurate records of the experience of starting the new group, for reference in starting later groups.
9. Build in monitoring and evaluation procedures for the first nine months.

every city, and in every countryside throughout the world where people can hear and see demonstrated the Gospel by their own intimates, in their own tongue, and thus have a reasonable opportunity to become disciples of Jesus Christ."[2]

The Great Commission cannot be fulfilled in this country with the number of churches that exist. In fact, the 310,000 churches in America today could double without overchurching the country. Can this really be true, when almost every community in America appears to be well-churched, with innumerable church buildings and open doors almost everywhere? One tends to conclude that there are plenty of churches in America, plenty of empty seats, plenty of room for everyone. Such a conclusion needs to be challenged. While it may seem that there are enough churches for everyone, enormous numbers of people are unchurched and will remain so if we expect existing churches to reach them. The reason is that there are many people in America who simply will not feel comfortable in existing churches. Different churches appeal to different kinds of people. And there are segments of people in nearly every part of the country to whom no existing church provides an attractive alternative for their lives. Or to say it another way, your church will not appeal to every person in your community, nor will any other.

The solution to this problem is not to hope other churches in the area will respond to the unique needs of these "unreachable" people. The secret is to identify who these people are and start a church structured to reach them.

Figure 4 presents some important insights into both the cost and the effectiveness of disciple-making endeavors with various homogeneous groups of people in your community. The closer the group is to the center circle, the less costly and more effective disciple-making efforts by members of your church will be. The farther the group is from the center circle, the costlier and less effective will be your disciple-making endeavors. By the time disciple-making efforts are focused on people in the far circles, the evangelism process has become one of missions. And every good missionary knows that the most effective strategy is to reach receptive people, plant a new church among those people, and then assist them in reaching their families and webs. Such a church among this group of people changes

Figure 4

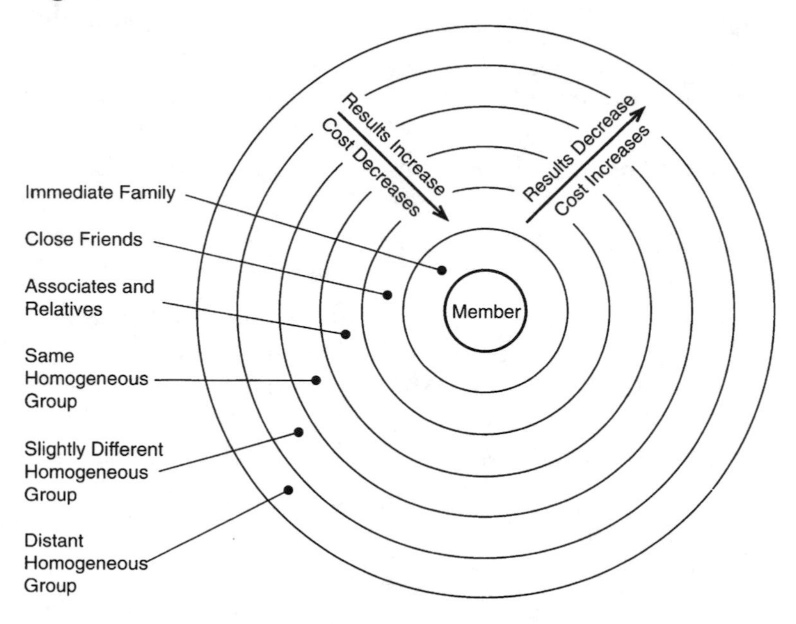

the process of disciple making from missions back to "near neighbor" and returns the group to the center of the circle (resulting in greater effectiveness).

Many churches like to think of themselves as being patterned after the New Testament church, as doing things in a biblical fashion. But is a church really a New Testament church if it isn't planting churches? Being a New Testament church means believing and doing what the New Testament church did. The New Testament church was concerned with, engaged in, and successful at establishing new congregations. Churches were planted in Jerusalem, Judea, Samaria, Galilee, Antioch, Rome, in city after city around the Mediterranean. Toward the end of his life, Paul was heading toward Spain to begin planting churches there. Church multiplication was an essential part of New

Testament life. Today, in a world in which three out of four people have yet to believe in Jesus Christ, if a congregation is not reproducing, it is not a New Testament church, no matter what it calls itself.

Church planting begins with the conviction that it is God's will that his church grow. Such a conviction grows into a deep concern for people in the community who are without Christ. When these concerns permeate the people of God in the local congregation, beginning a new church becomes a real possibility.

Most churches discover that planting a daughter church does not drain the resources of the mother church as much as they thought it would. Rather, it often proves to be a boost to growth, morale, and enthusiasm. Like the birth of a new baby, a brand-new congregation is a joy to experience.

If the people in North America are going to be reached for Christ, existing churches not only need to grow but need to give priority to the multiplication of new churches.

Begin thinking about planned parenthood in your church. Why not one every nine months?

5. Reach across Cultures

The Great Commission Christ gave to his church was a command to disciple "to the ends of the earth." Most English versions translate the command of Christ in Matthew 28:19 to read, "Make disciples of all the nations." But this is a mistranslation. The original Greek translation is to disciple *panta ta ethne.* Ethne does not mean the modern nation states, such as India, the United States, or China. Ethne means the ethnic units of humankind—all the different kinds of people in a nation, the variety of levels and subcultures of society. The Great Commission is a call to disciple every piece of the vast mosaic of humankind that are the three billion yet to believe.

In referring to his own call, Paul wrote, "This gospel . . . is about Jesus Christ our Lord. Through him I received the privilege of a commission . . . to lead to faith and obedience men [of all ethne]" (Rom. 1:1–5 NEB). The Great Commission will be fulfilled when every person has had a reasonable opportunity to see and hear the gospel from his or her intimates, in his or her culture and language, and is given a chance to become part of a local body of Christ.

A church concerned with responding to the Great Commission will indeed direct its attention to the people in its Potential Congregation. But it will not be able to overlook the vast numbers of people yet to hear and yet to be reached beyond the perimeters of its own small part of the world.

Missions should be a priority of any church concerned with the Great Commission. A special missions coordinator or committee should be found in every church to frequently keep the worldwide task in front of the congregation. Regular sermons, Sunday school lessons, speakers, films, and reports on missions projects are valuable. Consider adopting a special missions project if you do not have one. Encourage people in the church to visit that missions project. Perhaps sponsor a biannual church tour to the missions project and help raise money for members to go.

Christians today have the responsibility as no generation before to invest time, money, and people to reach out to "the ends of the earth" with the Good News.

Can the Great Commission be fulfilled? We have come a long way since Christ left those few apostles with such a seemingly impossible task. Now there are faithful Christians on every continent of the globe. There are Christian churches found in every country. It is not a question of whether the Great Commission can be fulfilled. It *is* being fulfilled. The question is whether you and your church will be a part of it. Will the Master return, as Christ illustrated in the parable of the talents, to find that your church has

hidden its treasure and has nothing to show? Or will he return to find the treasure left in your care to be multiplied through faithful investment, so he will then say to you, "Well done, thou good and faithful servant"?

Mark Peters and his friend Bob Taylor walked down the steps of the high school. It was a Friday evening. Mark and Bob had just finished playing in the church league basketball playoffs, helping their church to its first championship. They were exhilarated and exhausted as they headed toward their cars.

"Man, what a game!" said Mark.

"Yeah. What a season! Remember that first game?" laughed Bob.

"Don't remind me. Boy, did we get blown out of there."

"Well, we sure got our act together after that."

"You're coming to the celebration over at the church, aren't you?" asked Mark.

"Well, I . . . I don't know," stammered Bob.

"Hey, come on," insisted Mark. "We couldn't have made it through the season without you."

"Well, okay. But I've got to get going soon."

"Great. I'll see you over there," said Mark as they each got in their car.

Mark had been a member of the church for nearly a year. He had been introduced to Christ by his brother-in law, Jim Herman. Jim, as it turned out, had been reached through a fishing buddy named Pete. And of course, Pete was Chuck Bradley's first Extended Family member to come to Christ and the church.

So Mark was the fourth generation tracing his spiritual roots back to Chuck's involvement, over three years earlier, in The Master's Plan. Even though they were in the same church, Chuck would probably never know that he had been indirectly responsible for Mark's Christian commitment and involvement in the church or that Bob Taylor, now a member of Mark's Extended Family, would soon respond to the caring of the church and the body.

Since those first days of The Master's Plan, when Pastor Austin began meeting with various members and helping them share God's love with their Extended Families, the church had seen considerable new vitality and growth. In fact, a new committee had been organized during the previous week to examine the possibility of planting a new church in the coming year. The existing facilities were getting cramped, and the church had already started a second service.

What had happened to this church in the last three years? How and why did it move from an average church doing basically average church work to a dedicated and growing church equipping its lay members to fulfill the Great Commission in their world?

The secret was in laity mobilized for making disciples. Chuck's church had discovered that the key to reaching its world for Christ was in laypeople convinced (1) that the opportunity existed all about them and (2) that they could, individually and as a church, expect to see their friends, relatives, and associates become Christians and members of their church.

It was not just because they had read a book or participated in a special series of meetings. The reason Chuck's church began to realize its previously untapped possibilities was because the members had taken seriously the important biblical insights, as well as modern-day applications, of how Christ's Good News can be extended to the "remotest part of the earth." The laity had learned to communicate Christ's love and were using their natural networks for the expansion of his church.

Of course, there was not a 100 percent success rate. Not all the members of the church who could have been were involved in making disciples. Some Extended Family members never found Christ or his love through the church. A few new members of the church dropped out through oversights in the church incorporation system. But as Chuck, Pete, and several others on the church board were discussing at the last meeting, the events that took place three years previously, which launched the new emphasis in equipping laity and making disciples, had marked a new direction for the church. Those events had contributed directly to a new level of morale among the members, and the beginning of exciting new heights of achievement for the congregation in fulfilling Christ's command to go and make disciples.

Notes

Introduction

1. See Acts 1:15; 2:41, 47; 4:4; 5:14; 6:1, 7; 9:31; 11:21; 16:5; 21:20.

2. Leith Anderson, *A Church for the Twenty-First Century* (Minneapolis: Bethany, 1992), 190.

3. Arthur Glasser, *Why Church Growth?* (Monrovia, Calif.: Church Growth, Inc., 1984), audiotape recording.

4. Win Arn, *The Pastor's Church Growth Handbook,* vol. 1 (Monrovia, Calif.: Church Growth, Inc., 1979), 151–54.

Chapter 1: The Master's Plan: Making Disciples

1. George Peters, *A Theology of Church Growth* (Grand Rapids: Zondervan, 1981), 190.

2. Win Arn Productions, *The Great Commission Sunday School* (Monrovia, Calif.: Church Growth, Inc., 1986), videotape recording.

3. Michael Green, *Evangelism in the Early Church* (Grand Rapids: Eerdmans, 1970), 210.

4. Peters, *A Theology of Church Growth,* 219, 223.

5. Green, *Evangelism in the Early Church,* 35–36.

Chapter 2: How New Disciples Are Made: The *Oikos* Factor

1. Elmer Towns, *Evangelism and Church Growth* (Ventura, Calif.: Regal, 1995), 219.

2. Hans Walter Wolff, *Anthology of the Old Testament* (Philadelphia: Fortress Press, 1974), 215.

3. Cornell Goerner, *All Nations in God's Purpose* (Nashville: Broadman, 1979), 23.

4. Kenneth Scott Latourette, *A History of the Expansion of Christianity,* vol. 1, *The First Five Centuries* (New York: Harper, 1937), 116.

5. Donald McGavran, *Bridges of God* (New York: Friendship Press, 1968), 27.

6. Ibid., 27–28.

7. Win Arn Productions, *But . . . I'm Just a Layman* (Monrovia, Calif.: Church Growth, Inc., 1988), videotape recording.

8. Green, *Evangelism in the Early Church,* 210.

Chapter 3: Key Principles of Disciple Making

1. Win Arn, *The Church Growth Ratio Book* (Monrovia, Calif.: Church Growth Press, 1990), 52.

2. Hazel Felleman, ed., *Best Loved Poems of the American People* (New York: Garden City, 1936), 521–22.

3. Edward A. Rauff, *Why People Join the Church* (New York: Pilgrim Press, 1979), 115.

4. Syndicated news report, KFWB, Los Angeles, June 4, 1995.

5. Peter Hammond, *Cultural and Social Anthropology: Selected Readings* (New York: Macmillan, 1964), 145–46.

Chapter 4: Seven Steps for Making Disciples

1. Alan McGinnis, *The Friendship Factor* (Minneapolis: Augsburg, 1979), 109.

2. T. Holmes and R. Rahe, Holmes-Rahe Social Readjustment Scale, *The Journal of Psychosomatic Research* 2, 213–18.

3. Becky Tirabassi, *Wild Things Happen When I Pray* (Grand Rapids: Zondervan, 1993), 57.

4. Wayne McDill, *Making Friends for Christ* (Nashville: Broadman, 1979), 96.

Chapter 5: How to Reach Your Extended Family

1. David Augsburger, *Caring Enough to Confront* (Scottsdale, Ariz.: Herald Press, 1980), 127, 138.

2. Paul Cedar, *Seven Keys to Maximum Communication* (Wheaton: Tyndale House, 1980), 71.

3. Augsburger, *Caring Enough to Confront*, 138.

4. Paul Little, *How to Give Away Your Faith* (Downers Grove, Ill.: InterVarsity Press, 1966), 52.

5. McGinnis, *The Friendship Factor*, 54.

6. Ibid., 55.

7. McDill, *Making Friends for Christ*, 53.

8. Flavil Yeakley, "Research and the Growing Church," *Church Growth: America* (January-February 1981): 10.

9. Merlin Carothers, *Power in Praise* (Plainfield, N.J.: Logos International, 1972), 117.

10. P. T. Forsyth, *The Principle of Authority* (Independence, Mo.: Independence Press, 1952), 127.

11. Charles Arn, Donald McGavran, and Win Arn, *Growth: A New Vision for the Sunday School* (Monrovia, Calif.: Church Growth, Inc., 1980), 72.

12. Archibald Hunter, *Introducing the New Testament*, 3d ed. (Philadelphia: Westminster Press, 1972), 23–24.

13. Steven Smalley, "Conversion in the New Testament," in *The Churchman* 78, no. 3 (1979): 193–210.

14. Tirabassi, *Wild Things Happen When I Pray*, 36.

15. Yeakley, "Research and the Growing Church," 10.

16. Glasser, *Why Church Growth?* part 2.

17. Little, *How to Give Away Your Faith*, 53.

18. Arn, *The Pastor's Church Growth Handbook*, 44–60.

19. Samuel Southard, *Pastoral Evangelism* (Atlanta: John Knox Press, 1981), 27.

20. Keith Miller, *Living the Adventure* (Waco: Word, 1975), 102.

Chapter 6: Your Church: Partner in Disciple Making

1. Peters, *A Theology of Church Growth*, 240.

2. "The Master's Plan Church Action Kit" has excellent and specific ideas to raise the disciple-making awareness of laity in a local congregation. Information on the kit is available from Church Growth, Inc., P.O. Box 541, Monrovia, CA 91017.

3. Donald McGavran and Win Arn, *How to Grow a Church* (Glendale, Calif.: Regal, 1973), 36.

4. Flavil Yeakley, *Why Churches Grow* (Arvada, Colo.: Christian Communications, 1979), 66.

5. Lyle Schaller, interviewed by the authors, Pasadena, Calif., January 1982.

6. Win Arn, "Mass Evangelism: The Bottom Line," *Church Growth: America* (January-February 1978): 4.

7. Rodney Stark and William Bainbridge, "Recruitment to Cults and Sects," *American Journal of Sociology* 85, no. 6 (1981): 1376–95.

8. Ernest Eberhard, "How to Share the Message with Your Neighbors," *The Ensign* (June 1974): 6–11.

Chapter 7: Incorporating New Disciples into the Church

1. Lyle Schaller, *Assimilating New Members* (Nashville: Abingdon Press, 1978), 76.

2. Yeakley, *Why Churches Grow*, 44.

3. W. Charles Arn, "The Friendship Factor," *The Growth Report* (November-December 1992): 12.

4. "Lake Avenue Philosophy of Ministry," Lake Avenue Congregational Church, Pasadena, California.

5. George G. Hunter III, *Church for the Unchurched* (Nashville: Abingdon Press, 1996), 43.

Chapter 8: The Master's Plan: To the Ends of the Earth

1. "Growing Ideas," *Church Growth: America* 8, no. 3, 15.

2. Donald McGavran and Win Arn, *Ten Steps for Church Growth* (New York: Harper and Row, 1977), 21.

Win Arn is founder of Church Growth, Inc. He is the author of more than a dozen books and producer of numerous films and videos. As a respected church leader, Dr. Arn has led seminars and training sessions for clergy and laity around the world.

W. Charles Arn is president of Church Growth, Inc., a research, development, and consulting organization specializing in congregational ministry and growth. Dr. Arn is a widely respected authority in the field of congregational growth strategy. He is a graduate of Seattle Pacific University and earned his doctorate at the University of Southern California.
